BEST PRACTICE FOR THE TOEIC® L&R TEST
–Basic–

TOEIC® L&R TESTへの
総合アプローチ ―ベーシック―

YOSHIZUKA Hiroshi

Graham Skerritt

SEIBIDO

写真提供: © iStockPhoto
イラスト: 黒丸恭介
図版: 藤野伸芳

音声ファイルのダウンロード／ストリーミング

CD マーク表示がある箇所は、音声を弊社 HP より無料でダウンロード／ストリーミングすることができます。下記 URL の書籍詳細ページに音声ダウンロードアイコンがございますのでそちらから自習用音声としてご活用ください。

http://seibido.co.jp/ad605

BEST PRACTICE FOR THE TOEIC® L&R TEST
—Basic—

はしがき

　よくTOEICはビジネス英語と言われることがあります。しかし、これは正確にテストを言い表していません。実際には誰もが日常生活で遭遇するような実用的な内容で構成されています。つまり、普通の大人なら誰でも知っているような語彙、内容でできています。ですからTOEICを学べば実践的な日常英語を身に付けることができると言えます。TOEICのテスト勉強と思わず、使える英語を身に付けるという気持ちで取り組みましょう。

　それでは、そのような日常的な内容なのに、なぜTOEICは難しく感じるのでしょう。その答えは「スピード」と「分量」です。中学や高校ではTOEICの「スピード」はまず求められていませんし、「分量」も限られた時間にこんなにたくさん英語を「聞き」、「読む」ことが求められていないのです。一言で言えば「慣れていない」だけなのです。

　「慣れていない」受験者が何をすればよいか。それはリスニングもリーディングも「概要をつかむ」ことから始めます。この時のキーワードは「What, Where, Who」の3つです。よく5W1Hと言われますが、そんなに欲張るのはやめましょう。3つで十分です。話し手が「誰」で、「どこ」で、「何」について話しているのか、これが分かれば自分で満点をつけましょう。

　例えば、「レストラン (=Where) で店員と客 (=Who) が話していて席がいっぱいだと断られている (=What)」これだけ聞き取れれば満点です。

　例えば、「Eメールで会社の担当者 (=Who) がパーティー用に注文した食べ物の内容を変更したい (=What) と会社 (=Where) から送信したこと」が分かれば満点です。

　本書ではリスニングでもリーディングでもどんどん満点を取って「成功体験」を得られる工夫がなされています。「おお、聞き取れた」、「あ、何が書いてあるか分かった」という体験を積み重ねていってください。その連続で少しずつ難しい内容に挑戦していくうちに、いつの間にかTOEIC対策は終わっていますし、日常英語が身に付いています。

　本書で学ばれた皆さんが、「少しだけ自信が付いてきた」と感じられたら幸いです。

　最後になりましたが、前作『BEST PRACTICE FOR THE TOEIC LISTENING AND READING TEST-REVISED EDITION』のBasic版を作りましょう、とお声掛けくださった成美堂の佐野英一郎氏、また数々のアドバイスとともに編集の労をお取りくださった宍戸貢、佐野泰一のご両名に心から感謝申し上げます。

2020年秋

吉塚　弘

Graham Skerritt

本書の構成と使い方

■全般:

- 全UnitがRestaurantsやEntertainmentなどのトピック別の構成になっています。

- 各Unitには、Part 1〜Part 7までのすべてが収められています。

- 全UnitをHop, Step, Jumpと3分割、選択肢の数を徐々に増やすことで難易度が上がるようになっています。設問の数や選択肢の数がTOEICと異なりますので注意しましょう。Unitが進むに従って、徐々に実際のテストに近い構成になっています。

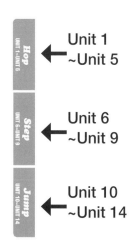

▶Warm up – Dictation Practice:

- リスニングセクションに入る前の耳慣らしです。

- 音声は成美堂ホームページ(https://www.seibido.co.jp)よりパソコンへダウンロード、あるいはスマートフォンやタブレットでストリーミング再生してください。

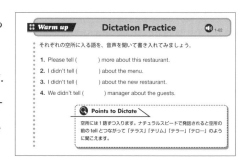

- 日本人にとって聞き取りにくい音変化を取りあげています。聞き取りの際のポイントは、"Points to Dictate"にあります。

☞音声を聞き、空所部分を書き取ってください。音声は何度聞いても構いません。さらに聞き取ったセンテンスを繰り返し発話します。発話できる音は必ず聞き取れるようになります。

▶頻出単語チェック！:

- 各Unitのトピックに頻出し、必修の単語（語彙）を抽出しました。

- 見出し語と意味のマッチングをするタスクになっています。

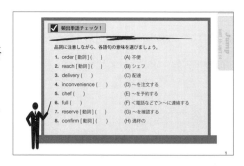

▶各Partの構成
LISTENING SECTION

全Partに"Check Point!"があります。何を学ぶのか、どのようなことに注意したらよいのか、を示しました。

- Part 1は、He, She, The man, The woman, Theyなどの主語と頻出する動詞を取り上げています。頻出の人物が主語の例で練習します。

- Part 2は、質問文に頻出する疑問詞を中心とした構成になっています。

- Part 3は、会話の概要を問う質問文で構成されています。What, Where, Whoがキーワードです。何について、どこで、誰と誰が話し合っているのかを大きく掴みます。3名の会話や図表を使った会話も後半に含まれています。

- Part 4は、説明文の主旨や主題、目的などの概略を問う質問で構成されています。Part 3同様What, Where, Whoを聞き取ります。

▶Grammar Review:

- 文法項目を頻度順に復習します。続くPart 5と6にはこの内容が盛り込まれています。

☞各項目の説明を読み、続く例題に取り組みます。

READING SECTION

Part 5　　　　　　　　Part 6　　　　　　　　Part 7

- Part 5は、4つの問題のうち、最初の2つが直前のGrammar Reviewで確認した内容を扱った文法問題、残りの2問が品詞別の語彙問題です。

- Part 6は、Unit 9までは2つの空所のうち、1つはGrammar Reviewで学んだ内容を反映した文法問題で、もう1つは語彙問題です。Unit 10からは3問となり文挿入問題となっています。

- Part 7は、出題頻度の高いEメールやメモ、手紙、広告文などを取り上げています。それぞれの説明文の主旨や主題、目的などの概略を問う質問文で構成されています。テキストメッセージやオンラインチャット形式の問題も含まれています。

🔊 マークの隣にある番号が、ダウンロード音声のトラック番号です。教室では教員の指示に従ってください。また、課外では、Warm upの音声と同じように成美堂ホームページよりPCへダウンロード、あるいはスマートフォンやタブレットでストリーミング再生して聞き取れなかった箇所を確実に聞き取れるようになるまで繰り返し聞いてください。

その他、Web英語学習システムのLINGUAPORTA(リンガポルタ)に対応しており、パソコンやスマートフォンを使ったモバイル・ラーニングが可能ですので、授業の復習等に役立ててください。

LINGUAPORTA

リンガポルタのご案内

> **リンガポルタ連動テキストをご購入の学生さんは、「リンガポルタ」を無料でご利用いただけます！**

　本テキストで学習していただく内容に準拠した問題を、オンライン学習システム「リンガポルタ」で学習していただくことができます。PC だけでなく、スマートフォンやタブレットでも学習できます。単語や文法、リスニング力などをよりしっかり身に付けていただくため、ぜひ積極的に活用してください。

　リンガポルタの利用にはアカウントとアクセスコードの登録が必要です。登録方法については下記ページにアクセスしてください。

https://www.seibido.co.jp/linguaporta/register.html

本テキスト「BEST PRACTICE FOR THE TOEIC(R) L&R TEST -Basic-」のアクセスコードは下記です。

7232-2045-1231-0365-0003-006e-Z4LF-C981

・リンガポルタの学習機能（画像はサンプルです。また、すべてのテキストに以下の 4 つの機能が用意されているわけではありません）

●多肢選択

●空所補充（音声を使っての聞き取り問題も可能）

●単語並びかえ（マウスや手で単語を移動）

●マッチング（マウスや手で単語を移動）

目　次

1 Restaurants

Hop
UNIT 1~UNIT 5

Step
UNIT 6~UNIT 9

Jump
UNIT 10~UNIT 14

:: **Warm up** **Dictation Practice** 1-02

それぞれの空所に入る語を、音声を聞いて書き入れてみましょう。

1. Please tell (   ) more about this restaurant.

2. I didn't tell (   ) about the menu.

3. I didn't tell (   ) about the new restaurant.

4. We didn't tell (   ) manager about the guests.

 Points to Dictate

空所には1語ずつ入ります。ナチュラルスピードで発話されると空所の
前の tell とつながって「テラス」「テリム」「テラー」「テロー」のよう
に聞こえます。

✓ 頻出単語チェック！

品詞に注意しながら、各語句の意味を選びましょう。

1. order [動詞] (   )   (A) 不便

2. reach [動詞] (   )   (B) シェフ

3. delivery (   )   (C) 配達

4. inconvenience (   )   (D) 〜を注文する

5. chef (   )   (E) 〜を予約する

6. full (   )   (F) <電話などで>〜に連絡する

7. reserve [動詞] (   )   (G) 〜を確認する

8. confirm [動詞] (   )   (H) 満杯の

PART 1 写真描写問題 1-03, 04

> *Check Point!* 人物の動作について説明される問題を見てみましょう。
> She's ～ ing in a restaurant.

それぞれの写真について、2つの説明文のうち適切なものを1つずつ選びましょう。

1. **2.**

(A) (B)   (A) (B)

PART 2 応答問題 1-05-07

> *Check Point!* 頻出の疑問文による質問文を見てみましょう。
> What time does this restaurant close?

それぞれの質問の応答として最も適切なものを1つずつ選びましょう。

3. Mark your answer on your answer sheet.   (A) (B)

4. Mark your answer on your answer sheet.   (A) (B)

5. Mark your answer on your answer sheet.   (A) (B)

PART 3　会話問題　　　　　　　　　　　1-08, 09

Check Point!　2人が「どこで会話をしているか」聞き取りましょう。
Where most likely are the speakers?

会話についての設問に対し、最も適切なものを1つずつ選びましょう。

6. Where most likely are the speakers?

(A) At a supermarket

(B) At a restaurant

7. What problem does the woman mention?

(A) The place is closed.

(B) The place is very busy.

PART 4　説明文問題　　　　　　　　　　　1-10, 11

Check Point!　話者は「どこで働いているか」聞き取りましょう。
Where does the speaker most likely work?

説明文についての設問に対し、最も適切なものを1つずつ選びましょう。

8. Where does the speaker most likely work?

(A) At a university

(B) At a restaurant

9. What is the main purpose of the message?

(A) To explain why the restaurant is closed

(B) To promote Free-Drink Day

Hop　UNIT 1~UNIT 5

Step　UNIT 6~UNIT 9

Jump　UNIT 10~UNIT 14

人称代名詞には、それぞれ「主格」「所有格」「目的格」という３つの「格」と「所有代名詞」があります。また、それぞれの人称には単数と複数があります。下の表で見直してみましょう。

人称代名詞の一覧表				
	主格	所有格	目的格	所有代名詞
１人称単数	I	my	me	mine
２人称単数	you	your	you	yours
３人称単数（男性）	he	his	him	his
３人称単数（女性）	she	her	her	hers
３人称単数（人間以外）	it	its	it	—
１人称複数	we	our	us	ours
２人称複数	you	your	you	yours
３人称複数	they	their	them	theirs

< 例題 > 各空所に入れるべき最も適切な語を１つずつ選びなさい。

① ------ is the manager of the restaurant.

　(A) He　　(B) His　　(C) Him

② He works in the restaurant with ------ wife.

　(A) he　　(B) his　　(C) him

③ His wife likes ------.

　(A) he　　(B) his　　(C) him

④ The restaurant is not ------.

　(A) he　　(B) him　　(C) his

・主格は文の主語になります。(例) He is a manager.
・所有格は名詞を所有します。(例) His wife
・目的格は目的語として使われます。(例) She likes him.
・所有代名詞は「〜のもの」という意味になります。(例) It's his.

Reading Section

Hop
UNIT 1~UNIT 5

Step
UNIT 6~UNIT 9

Jump
UNIT 10~UNIT 14

PART 5 短文穴埋め問題

Check Point!

文法問題：人称代名詞、語彙問題：動詞
人称代名詞なら空所に入れるべき「格」を見極めましょう。

それぞれの空所に入れるのに最も適切なものを1つずつ選びましょう。

10. Our head chef, Bill Patton, is very friendly, but please don't talk to him while ------- is cooking.

(A) he   (B) his

11. We asked the restaurant owner to change ------- table to the window side right away.

(A) us   (B) our

12. Our restaurant is always really busy at lunchtime, so you cannot ------- a table.

(A) reserve   (B) reach

13. Please ask one of our staff when you are ready to ------- your food.

(A) stay   (B) order

12. 13. は動詞の選択問題です。文意からどちらの動詞が適切か選びましょう。
選択肢を見て、品詞など何が問われているかを見極めることも大切です。

Check Point! E-mail
文法問題：人称代名詞、語彙問題：動詞

それぞれの空所に入れるのに最も適切なものを1つずつ選びましょう。

To: Fred Richards <frichards@freenet.com>

From: Ann Walker <awalker@bestpizza.com>

Date: April 10

Subject: Our New Delivery Service

Dear Fred,

We would like to announce that Best Pizza will start a delivery service from next month. You will get your order within 30 minutes. If not, we will ------- the money to you. Plus, for all customers who receive this
14.
e-mail, we will deliver a free medium-size pizza on ------- birthday.
15.
For more details, please call 123-4567-8901.

Best regards,

Ann Walker
Best Pizza

---

14. (A) forget

(B) return

15. (A) you

(B) your

PART 7　読解問題

Check Point!　E-mail －1つの文書
メールの Subject には主旨が凝縮されていることを確認
しましょう。

文章を読んで、それぞれの設問の答えとして最も適切なものを1つずつ選びましょう。

Hop
UNIT 1~UNIT 5

Step
UNIT 6~UNIT 9

Jump
UNIT 10~UNIT 14

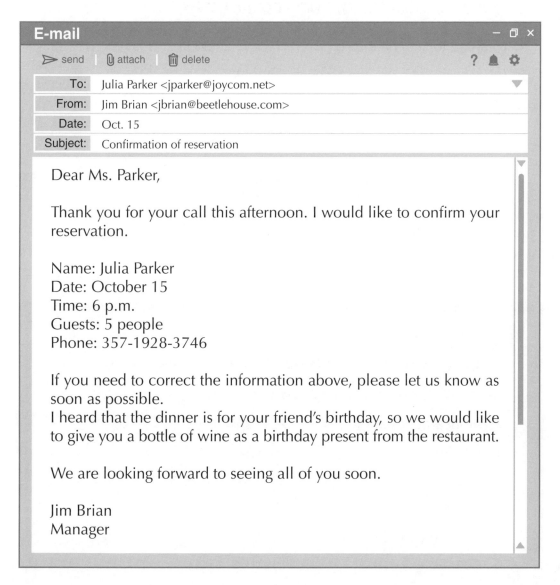

E-mail　　　　　　　　　　　　　　　　　　－ ☐ ✕

➤ send　　📎 attach　　🗑 delete　　　　　　　? 🔔 ⚙

To:	Julia Parker <jparker@joycom.net>	▼
From:	Jim Brian <jbrian@beetlehouse.com>	
Date:	Oct. 15	
Subject:	Confirmation of reservation	

Dear Ms. Parker,

Thank you for your call this afternoon. I would like to confirm your reservation.

Name: Julia Parker
Date: October 15
Time: 6 p.m.
Guests: 5 people
Phone: 357-1928-3746

If you need to correct the information above, please let us know as soon as possible.
I heard that the dinner is for your friend's birthday, so we would like to give you a bottle of wine as a birthday present from the restaurant.

We are looking forward to seeing all of you soon.

Jim Brian
Manager

---

16. What is the purpose of the e-mail?

　(A) To confirm a reservation

　(B) To promote a restaurant

17. Where does Mr. Brian most likely work?

　(A) At a hotel

　(B) At a restaurant

UNIT

2 Entertainment

Warm up　　**Dictation Practice**　 1-12

それぞれの空所に入る語を、音声を聞いて書き入れてみましょう。

1. I wanted to see the movie (　　　　　　) I couldn't.

2. (　　　　　　) I go to the amusement park?

3. (　　　　　　) I read this comic?

4. (　　　　　　) I borrow your video game?

> 🔍 **Points to Dictate**
>
> 空所には１語ずつ入ります。ナチュラルスピードで発話されると空所の
> 後の I とつながって「バライ」「カナイ」「シュライ」「クライ」のよう
> に聞こえます。

✅ **頻出単語チェック！**

各語句の意味を **(A)** 〜 **(H)** から選びましょう。

1. amusement park (　　) 　　(A) 博物館

2. museum (　　) 　　(B) 男優

3. stage (　　) 　　(C) ＜物事＞に興味に興味がある

4. actor (　　) 　　(D) 遊園地

5. starring [動詞] (　　) 　　(E) 式

6. ceremony (　　) 　　(F) 出来事

7. be interested in (　　) 　　(G) 舞台

8. event (　　) 　　(H) ＜俳優など＞を主演させる

Listening Section

PART 1　写真描写問題

 1-13, 14

Check Point!　人物の動作について説明される問題を見てみましょう。
He's ～ ing TV.

それぞれの写真について、2つの説明文のうち適切なものを1つずつ選びましょう。

1.

Ⓐ Ⓑ

2.

Ⓐ Ⓑ

PART 2　応答問題

 1-15-17

Check Point!　頻出の疑問文による質問文を見てみましょう。
Did you watch TV last night?

それぞれの質問の応答として最も適切なものを1つずつ選びましょう。

3. Mark your answer on your answer sheet.　　Ⓐ Ⓑ

4. Mark your answer on your answer sheet.　　Ⓐ Ⓑ

5. Mark your answer on your answer sheet.　　Ⓐ Ⓑ

Hop
UNIT 1～UNIT 5

Step
UNIT 6～UNIT 9

Jump
UNIT 10～UNIT 14

Check Point!   会話をしている「2人が誰なのか」大きく捉えましょう。
Who most likely are the speakers?

会話についての設問に対し、最も適切なものを1つずつ選びましょう。

6. Who most likely are the speakers?

(A) Coworkers

(B) College students

7. What does the woman say she will do?

(A) Buy him a hot dog

(B) Help the man with his report

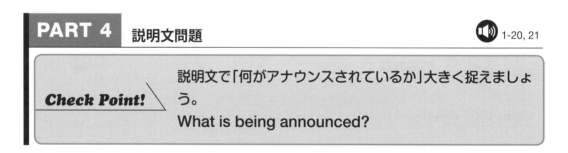

PART 4   説明文問題   1-20, 21

Check Point!   説明文で「何がアナウンスされているか」大きく捉えましょう。
What is being announced?

説明文についての設問に対し、最も適切なものを1つずつ選びましょう。

8. What is being announced?

(A) A new museum

(B) A new Web site

9. Who is Brian Lewis?

(A) A listener

(B) A movie star

Grammar Review 不定代名詞

不定代名詞とは、不特定の人やモノ、数量を漠然と表します。

1. Here are two sweaters. / She takes **one**. / He takes **the other**.
   ここにセーターが２枚あり、彼女が１枚をとります。彼はもう１枚のほうをとります。

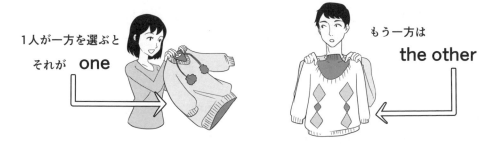

1人が一方を選ぶと　それが **one**

もう一方は **the other**

2. Here are nine sweaters. / She takes this **one**. / He takes **another**.
   ここに９枚のセーターがある。彼女はこれをとります。彼はほかのどれか１枚をとります。

3. I want all the others.
   私は残り全部が欲しいです。

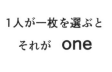

1人が一枚を選ぶと　それが **one**

他の一つひとつは **another**
an + other → another

他はまとめて **the others**

< 例題 > 各空所に入れるべき最も適切な語を１つずつ選びなさい。

① I don't like this. Please show me ------.

　　(A) other　(B) another　(C) one

② Do you have a map? Yes, I have ------.

　　(A) one　(B) it　(C) another

③ I took this sandwich. Sue took all ------.

　　(A) one　(B) another　(C) the others

Reading Section

PART 5 短文穴埋め問題

Check Point! 文法問題：不定代名詞、語彙問題：動詞
不定代名詞は他の一方との関係を見極めましょう。

それぞれの空所に入れるのに最も適切なものを 1 つずつ選びましょう。

10. We have two kinds of tickets: ------- is for the first floor, and the other is for the second floor.

    (A) One   (B) None

11. There are five actors on the stage. Two are American and ------- are all British.

    (A) another   (B) the others

12. I ------- you watch this new action movie starring Allen Foster.

    (A) decide   (B) recommend

13. I started to ------- pictures when I was five.

    (A) draw   (B) write

12. 13. は動詞の選択問題です。文意からどちらの動詞が適切か選びましょう。
選択肢を見て、何が問われているかを見極めることも大切です。

PART 6　長文穴埋め問題

Hop
UNIT 1~UNIT 5

Step
UNIT 6~UNIT 9

Jump
UNIT 10~UNIT 14

Check Point! ＼ Notice
文法問題：不定代名詞、語彙問題：動詞

それぞれの空所に入れるのに最も適切なものを 1 つずつ選びましょう。

Volunteers Wanted

Greenville City Office is planning a Hot Jazz Night this August. We will ------- many famous jazz musicians, such as John Lewis and Kelly Adams.
14.
We are now looking for 30 volunteers to support the event. ------- who
15.
loves jazz can apply. If you are interested, please visit *www.gco.gov/*.

14. (A) catch

(B) invite

15. (A) Anybody

(B) Somebody

> *Check Point!* Article—1つの文書
> 「記事」は初めに結論や重要なメッセージがあります。

文章を読んで、それぞれの設問の答えとして最も適切なものを1つずつ選びましょう。

National Zoo Opens Next Month

Mayor John McGregor announced that the National Zoo will open on the first day of next month. It took almost five years to build the zoo, and the opening of the zoo was delayed for half a year because of construction problems. The zoo has 120 kinds of animals from 80 countries, so it is the largest zoo in the country. The mayor said he wants many people from all over the world to visit the zoo.

---

16. What is the purpose of the article?

(A) To announce the opening of a zoo

(B) To explain the kinds of animals at a zoo

17. Who is Mr. McGregor?

(A) The president of the zoo

(B) The mayor of the city

UNIT

3 Business

それぞれの空所に入る語を、音声を聞いて書き入れてみましょう。

1. I want (　　　)(　　　) visit our client with me.

2. I will (　　　)(　　　) Chicago on business tomorrow.

3. What (　　　)(　　　) do for a living?

4. What (　　　)(　　　) learn from the business magazine?

> ### 🔍 Points to Dictate
>
> 空所には１語ずつ入ります。ナチュラルスピードで発話されると空所の前後とつながって「ウォンチュル」「ゴル」「ワルユ」「ワッジュ」のように聞こえます。

✔ 頻出単語チェック！

品詞に注意しながら、各語句の意味を選びましょう。

1. document (　)   (A) 顧客
2. supplier (　)   (B) …のため
3. increase [動詞] (　)   (C) 卸売業者
4. customer (　)   (D) ～を遅らせる
5. ship [動詞] (　)   (E) ～を増やす
6. recruit [動詞] (　)   (F) 書類
7. delay [動詞] (　)   (G) ～を送る
8. due to … (　)   (H) ～を募集する

Listening Section

PART 1 　写真描写問題

 1-23, 24

Check Point! 　人物の動作について説明される問題を見てみましょう。
The woman is 〜 ing with the man.

それぞれの写真について、2つの説明文のうち適切なものを1つずつ選びましょう。

1.

Ⓐ Ⓑ

2.

Ⓐ Ⓑ

PART 2 　応答問題

 1-25-27

Check Point! 　頻出の疑問文による質問文を見てみましょう。
Which section is on the third floor?

それぞれの質問の応答として最も適切なものを1つずつ選びましょう。

3. Mark your answer on your answer sheet. 　Ⓐ Ⓑ

4. Mark your answer on your answer sheet. 　Ⓐ Ⓑ

5. Mark your answer on your answer sheet. 　Ⓐ Ⓑ

PART 3　会話問題 1-28, 29

Check Point!　会話で「何が問題となっているのか」大きく捉えましょう。
What is the problem?

会話についての設問に対し、最も適切なものを1つずつ選びましょう。

6. What is the problem?
(A) The shipment will be delayed.
(B) The order was cancelled.

7. Who most likely is the man?
(A) A supplier
(B) A customer

PART 4　説明文問題 1-30, 31

Check Point!　説明文のニュースリポートでは「何が主題か」大きく捉えましょう。
What is the main topic of the news report?

説明文についての設問に対し、最も適切なものを1つずつ選びましょう。

8. What is the main topic of the news report?
(A) A new factory
(B) A new Web site

9. What does the company want to do?
(A) Hire new people
(B) Build a Web site

再帰代名詞は「〜自身」を意味する語です。Unit 1で学んだ人称代名詞の「所有格」「目的格」に -self を付けます。

1人称、2人称では「人称代名詞の所有格*＋ self」ですが、3人称になると「人称代名詞の目的格*＋ self」です。（＊p.4参照）

	単数	複数
1人称	myself	ourselves
2人称	yourself	yourselves
3人称	himself, herself, itself	themselves

■再帰代名詞の3つの用法：1．強意用法 2．再帰用法 3．慣用的用法

1. The professional baseball player **himself** taught us baseball.
   そのプロ野球選手が自分で私たちに野球を教えてくれた。（「彼自身」を強調）

2. Eight-year-old Meg believes **herself** to be an adult.
   8歳の Meg は自分を大人だと信じている。

3. Did you build this house **by yourself**?
   あなたはこの家を自分で建てたのですか。（「自分ひとりで」という意味の慣用句）

< 例題 > 各空所に入れるべき最も適切な語を1つずつ選びなさい。

① I met the President of the United States ------ yesterday.

   (A) himself (B) his (C) he

② Azusa is unable to express ------ in English.

   (A) her (B) herself (C) hers

③ The old man lived in the big house by ------.

   (A) he (B) him (C) himself

Reading Section

Hop
UNIT 1～UNIT 5

Step
UNIT 6～UNIT 9

Jump
UNIT 10～UNIT 14

PART 5   短文穴埋め問題

Check Point!　文法問題：再帰代名詞、語彙問題：動詞
空所に入る代名詞を見極めましょう。ここでは直前の by
に注目します。

それぞれの空所に入れるのに最も適切なものを 1 つずつ選びましょう。

10. The president ------- met us at the train station.
(A) him   (B) himself

11. Mr. Williams had to buy his airplane ticket by ------- because his secretary
was absent yesterday.
(A) him   (B) himself

12. Mooz Clothing, Inc., decided to ------- the number of workers this year.
(A) invite   (B) increase

13. Our company ------- more than 100 e-mails from customers every day.
(A) receives   (B) carries

Check Point!

Article
文法問題：再帰代名詞、語彙問題：名詞

それぞれの空所に入れるのに最も適切なものを1つずつ選びましょう。

Mayor Turner to Sandeen: Choose Riverdale

Mayor Philip Turner ------- visited Sandeen Auto Company yesterday. He
14.
was there to ask them to build their new factory in Riverdale. After Foton
closed its car factory last year, Riverdale needs a new factory to give jobs
to local -------.
15.

---

14. (A) himself
(B) itself

15. (A) people
(B) factories

PART 7　読解問題

Check Point!
Web page ― 1 つの文書
タイトルや掲載者などは常に頭に入れておきましょう。

文章を読んで、それぞれの設問の答えとして最も適切なものを 1 つずつ選びましょう。

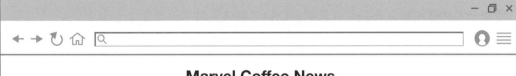

Marvel Coffee News

The CEO of Marvel Coffee, George Nelson, announced that it will open 60 new stores by the end of October. Marvel Coffee started out as a single store five years ago. Now it has 30 stores in Georgia. In a press release, Nelson also stated that to expand the number of stores, he will recruit franchise owners this month.

16. What is indicated about Marvel Coffee?

　　(A) It will increase the number of shops.

　　(B) It will open its first store this October.

17. Who is George Nelson?

　　(A) The owner of a coffee shop

　　(B) The president of the company

4 Office

Dictation Practice 1-32

それぞれの空所に入る語を、音声を聞いて書き入れてみましょう。

1. Shall I turn on the air conditioner? Yes, please turn (　　　)(　　　).

2. Shall I leave the copy machine on? Please turn (　　　)(　　　).

3. I haven't done it (　　　)(　　　).

4. Do you mind if I close the window? No, not (　　　)(　　　).

 Points to Dictate

空所には1語ずつ入ります。ナチュラルスピードで発話されると1. と2. は turn が空所の語とつながって「ターニロン」「ターニロフ」、3. は「アロール」、4. は not が空所とつながって「ノダロール」のように聞こえます。

✓ **頻出単語チェック！**

品詞に注意しながら、各語句の意味を選びましょう。

1. photocopy (　) 　　　　　(A) 総計

2. cancel [動詞] (　) 　　　(B) ～を共有する

3. report [動詞] (　) 　　　(C) ～を報告する

4. invite [動詞] (　) 　　　(D) 従業員

5. employee (　) 　　　　　(E) ～をキャンセルする

6. amount (　) 　　　　　　(F) コピー

7. share [動詞] (　) 　　　(G) ～を招く

8. sales (　) 　　　　　　　(H) 販売の

Listening Section

PART 1　写真描写問題

 1-33, 34

Check Point! | 人物の動作について説明される問題を見てみましょう。
The man is ～ ing on the computer.

それぞれの写真について、2つの説明文のうち適切なものを1つずつ選びましょう。

1.

Ⓐ Ⓑ

2.

Ⓐ Ⓑ

PART 2　応答問題

 1-35-37

Check Point! | 頻出の疑問文による質問文を見てみましょう。
Which office is yours?

それぞれの質問の応答として最も適切なものを1つずつ選びましょう。

3. Mark your answer on your answer sheet.　　Ⓐ Ⓑ

4. Mark your answer on your answer sheet.　　Ⓐ Ⓑ

5. Mark your answer on your answer sheet.　　Ⓐ Ⓑ

Hop
UNIT 1~UNIT 5

Step
UNIT 6~UNIT 9

Jump
UNIT 10~UNIT 14

PART 3 会話問題 1-38, 39

Check Point! 「2人がどこで会話をしているのか」大きく捉えましょう。
Where most likely are the speakers?

会話についての設問に対し、最も適切なものを1つずつ選びましょう。

6. Where most likely are the speakers?

(A) At an office

(B) At home

7. What does the woman say she will do?

(A) Work late

(B) Drive someone home

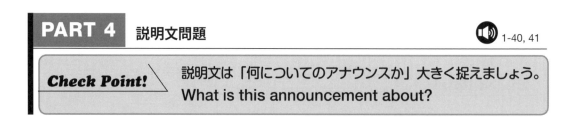

PART 4 説明文問題 1-40, 41

Check Point! 説明文は「何についてのアナウンスか」大きく捉えましょう。
What is this announcement about?

説明文についての設問に対し、最も適切なものを1つずつ選びましょう。

8. What is this announcement about?

(A) A repair

(B) A meeting

9. What does the speaker ask the listeners to do?

(A) Don't be noisy

(B) Clear the desks

Grammar Review 現在完了形

現在完了形は「have ＋過去分詞」で表される時制です。(→ have finish<u>ed</u>)

■完了（結果）、経験、継続と３つの用法があります。

1. **完了**（結果）は「やり終えた」という<u>動作の完了</u>を表します。現在の状況に焦点が置かれます。つまり現在宿題が終わった（完了した）ことがポイントです。

   I have just done the homework. (私は宿題をやり終えたところです)

   ずっと宿題をやっていたけど、「今それをやり終えた」という動作の完了です。

2. **経験**は「～したことがある」を表します。「過去にその経験があるかないか」現在の時点での経験が問われています。

   I have visited Fukuoka three times. (私は福岡に３度行ったことがある)

3. **継続**は「過去から現在まで同じ状態がずっと続くこと」を表します。

   I have lived in Osaka for ten years. (私は大阪に 10 年住んでいます [今現在も])

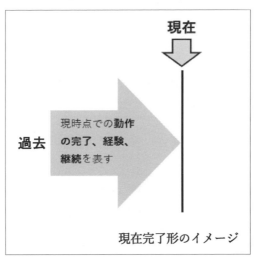

現在完了形のイメージ

< 例題 > 各空所に入れるべき最も適切な語を１つずつ選びなさい。

① I have ------ Jason for five years.

　(A) know　(B) knew　(C) known

② We have just ------ at Kyoto Station.

　(A) arrive　(B) arrived　(C) arriving

③ Saori has ------- Nagoya once.

　(A) visit　(B) visits　(C) visited

PART 5 短文穴埋め問題

Check Point! 文法問題：現在完了形、語彙問題：動詞
現在完了形の基本「have ＋過去分詞」を思い出しましょう。

それぞれの空所に入れるのに最も適切なものを1つずつ選びましょう。

10. We have ------- in this office for more than ten years.

(A) work　　　(B) worked

11. Most of our workers have never ------- our Vietnam office.

(A) visit　　　(B) visited

12. My boss asked me to ------- 15 copies of this document.

(A) make　　　(B) give

13. Lisa has ------- next Monday's section meeting.

(A) stopped　　(B) canceled

PART 6 長文穴埋め問題

Check Point! \ Notice
文法問題：現在完了形、語彙問題：動詞

それぞれの空所に入れるのに最も適切なものを 1 つずつ選びましょう。

To: All staff

From: Jessica Campbell

Date: March 10

Subject: Celebration dinner

Dear All,

Thank you all for your hard work this year.

I am delighted to report that we have ------- the year very strongly – sales
14.
are up almost 10% on last year.

So, to ------- our success, I would like to invite you all to a celebration
15.
dinner at the Grand Hotel on March 21. All food and drink will be paid
for by the company.

I hope to see you there.

Best wishes,

Jessica

---

14. (A) finish

(B) finished

15. (A) celebrate

(B) keep

> *Check Point!* Notice －1つの文書
> 「告知の目的が何か」大きく捉えましょう。

文章を読んで、それぞれの設問の答えとして最も適切なものを1つずつ選びましょう。

To All Roger's Foods Employees

As you know, this year our aim is to make the office completely paperless. However, over the past three months, the amount of copy paper used in the office was actually higher than the previous year. This is very disappointing, so we would like everyone to think of ways to cut down on their use of paper. For example, please share information by e-mail instead of printing documents.

Thank you for your kind cooperation.

General Affairs Dept.

16. What is the purpose of the notice?

  (A) To remind workers to use less papers

  (B) To say thank you to all workers

17. What will the workers most likely do next?

  (A) Try to share paper documents

  (B) Try to use as little paper as possible

5 Telephone

Hop
UNIT 1~UNIT 5

Step
UNIT 6~UNIT 9

Jump
UNIT 10~UNIT 14

:: **Warm up** | **Dictation Practice** 1-42

それぞれの空所に入る語を、音声を聞いて書き入れてみましょう。

1. Hi, Cindy. (   )(   )(   ) movie this Saturday?

2. Excuse me, but (   )(   )(   ) get to your office building?

3. Can you come back now? No, I'm (   )(   ) from the office.

4. Will you call back (   )(   )(   )?

> 🔍 **Points to Dictate**
>
> 空所には1語ずつ入ります。ナチュラルスピードで発話されると空所は
> 「ハバラ」「ハウルアイ」「ファラウェイ」「イナナワー」のように聞こえ
> ます。

✓ **頻出単語チェック!**

品詞に注意しながら、各語句の意味を選びましょう。

1. mobile phone (   )   (A) 利用者
2. exchange [動詞] (   )   (B) 携帯電話
3. user (   )   (C) 型
4. leave a message (   )   (D) ＜電話の＞内線
5. model (   )   (E) 電話をかけ返す
6. call back (   )   (F) メッセージを残す
7. extension (   )   (G) ～を交換する
8. screen (   )   (H) ＜携帯電話＞の画面

Listening Section

PART 1　写真描写問題 1-43, 44

> **Check Point!**　人物の動作について説明される問題を見てみましょう。
> The woman is ～ ing at her mobile phone.

それぞれの写真について、2つの説明文のうち適切なものを1つずつ選びましょう。

1.

Ⓐ Ⓑ

2.

Ⓐ Ⓑ

PART 2　応答問題 1-45-47

> **Check Point!**　頻出の疑問文による質問文を見てみましょう。
> Could you tell me your phone number?

それぞれの質問の応答として最も適切なものを1つずつ選びましょう。

3. Mark your answer on your answer sheet.　　Ⓐ Ⓑ

4. Mark your answer on your answer sheet.　　Ⓐ Ⓑ

5. Mark your answer on your answer sheet.　　Ⓐ Ⓑ

PART 3　会話問題 1-48, 49

Check Point!　なぜ男性は電話をかけているのか、その「理由」を聞き取りましょう。
Why is the man calling?

会話についての設問に対し、最も適切なものを１つずつ選びましょう。

6. Why is the man calling?

(A) To ask about delivering an item

(B) To ask about repairing an item

7. What does the woman say she will do with the hair dryer?

(A) Repair it

(B) Exchange it for a new one

PART 4　説明文問題 1-50, 51

Check Point!　電話に残されたメッセージです。発信人のお店の商売は何でしょう。
What does the store sell?

説明文についての設問に対し、最も適切なものを１つずつ選びましょう。

8. What does the store sell?

(A) Bikes

(B) Cards

9. Who is the announcement for?

(A) The store owner

(B) A customer

Hop UNIT 1〜UNIT 5

Step UNIT 6〜UNIT 9

Jump UNIT 10〜UNIT 14

■文中の「述語動詞の単数・複数はつねに文の主語に一致」することを表しています。

I **am** a student.
主語 述語

主語の "I"(一人称単数)が "We"(一人称複数)に変わると、述語動詞の am も are と変化します。これが「主語と動詞の一致」です。

We **are** students.
主語 述語

2人称：You are a student.

3人称：Souta is a student.

Souta and Aya are students. (Souta and Aya = They と考えます。)

■上記 be 動詞ではなく一般動詞の場合(現在形)を考えてみます。

3人称単数 　　Souta　　**speaks**　　Japanese.
　　　　　　　　　　動詞にsがつく

3人称**単**数で動詞は**現**在形。3単現です。

3人称複数　Souta and Aya　　　speak　　Japanese.

■応用編を考えてみましょう。

The meeting room with lots of windows ------ very hot in summer.

(窓の多い会議室は夏にはとても暑くなります)

☞この文では主語は The meeting room です。したがって、空所には gets が入ります。主語を修飾する語句 lots of windows に引きずられて get を入れないことです。つまり主語を見極めることが大切です。

< 例題 > 各空所に入れるべき最も適切な語を1つずつ選びなさい。

① Souta and Aya ------- in Sapporo.

(A) live　(B) lives　(C) living

② The souvenir shops in Kyoto ------- the same T-shirts.

(A) carry　(B) carries　(C) carrying

③ The shop with many T-shirts ------- some good postcards too.

(A) sell　(B) sells　(C) to sell

Reading Section

PART 5　短文穴埋め問題

Check Point!　文法問題：主語と動詞の一致、語彙問題：名詞
主語が単数か複数かを見極めて「動詞を選択」しましょう。

それぞれの空所に入れるのに最も適切なものを１つずつ選びましょう。

10. Mr. and Mrs. Brown ------- at the same telephone company.

(A) work　　　　　(B) works

11. The number of mobile phone users ------- increased rapidly.

(A) have　　　　　(B) has

12. I'm away from my desk right now, so please leave a ------- after the beep.

(A) word　　　　　(B) message

13. Mr. White wanted to talk to Ken directly, so he had to dial ------- 357.

(A) extension　　　(B) expression

Hop
UNIT 1~UNIT 5

Step
UNIT 6~UNIT 9

Jump
UNIT 10~UNIT 14

Check Point! Memo
文法問題：主語と動詞の一致、語彙問題：形容詞

それぞれの空所に入れるのに最も適切なものを 1 つずつ選びましょう。

Cathy,

Douglas Murphy from M&C Corporation called while you were out. Their sales team ------- to ask you some questions about the new SP-630 mobile
14.
phone. He said it was not -------, but please call him back later. His phone
15.
number is 357-020-5197.

James

---

14. (A) want

    (B) wants

15. (A) urgent

    (B) right

PART 7　読解問題

> **Check Point!** Advertisement ー1つの文書
> 何の広告でしょう。タイトルには常に目を通しましょう。

文章を読んで、それぞれの設問の答えとして最も適切なものを1つずつ選びましょう。

Free Wi-Fi with XP777 Mobile Phone

Are you satisfied with your mobile phone? Is it fast enough? Is the screen big enough? Does the battery last long enough? If not, now is a good time to buy the new XP777 – because we will give you six months of Wi-Fi for free!

Give us your old phone and you can get a discount. For more details, see: *www.mphone.com/newphone/promotion/*.

---

16. What is indicated by the advertisement?

(A) The new phone is not expensive.

(B) The new phone is fast and has a big screen.

17. What information is NOT given in the advertisement?

(A) The company URL

(B) The price of the new model

6 Letters & E-mails

それぞれの空所に入る語を、音声を聞いて書き入れてみましょう。

1. If you don't know the word, you can look (　　)(　　) in the dictionary.

2. I think I saw (　　)(　　) the e-mail.

3. Where's my birthday card? I put (　　)(　　) the table.

4. Let me read the e-mail. Wait a minute, I'll print (　　)(　　).

 Points to Dictate

空所には1語ずつ入ります。ナチュラルスピードで1. は look とつながって「ルッキラップ」2. は「イリン」3. は「プリロン」4. は「プリンティラウ」のように聞こえます。

✓ **頻出単語チェック！**

品詞に注意しながら、各語句の意味を選びましょう。

1. type [動詞] (　　)　　(A) 正式の

2. post [動詞] (　　)　　(B) 件名

3. stamp (　　)　　(C) 切手

4. formal (　　)　　(D) ～を投函する

5. e-mail [動詞] (　　)　　(E) ～に E- メールを送る

6. subject (　　)　　(F) ＜手紙などを＞タイプする

7. response (　　)　　(G) 返答

8. look forward to... (　　)　　(H) …を期待する

Listening Section

PART 1　写真描写問題

 1-53, 54

Check Point!　人物の動作について説明される問題を見てみましょう。
The man is ～ ing on the computer.

それぞれの写真について、3つの説明文のうち適切なものを1つずつ選びましょう。

1.

Ⓐ Ⓑ Ⓒ

2.

Ⓐ Ⓑ Ⓒ

PART 2　応答問題

 1-55-57

Check Point!　頻出の疑問文による質問文を見てみましょう。
Will you mail this letter for me?

それぞれの質問の応答として最も適切なものを1つずつ選びましょう。

3. Mark your answer on your answer sheet.　　Ⓐ Ⓑ Ⓒ

4. Mark your answer on your answer sheet.　　Ⓐ Ⓑ Ⓒ

5. Mark your answer on your answer sheet.　　Ⓐ Ⓑ Ⓒ

Check Point! この会話が「どこで話されているか」大きく捉えましょう。
Where does this conversation take place?

会話についての設問に対し、最も適切なものを1つずつ選びましょう。

6. Where does this conversation take place?

(A) At the post office

(B) At an office

(C) At home

7. What does the woman say she will do?

(A) Buy some stamps for the man

(B) Give the letter back to the man

(C) Mail a letter

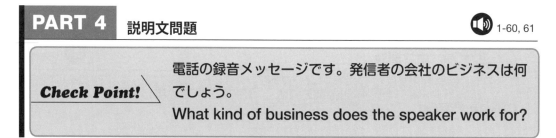

PART 4 説明文問題 1-60, 61

Check Point! 電話の録音メッセージです。発信者の会社のビジネスは何でしょう。
What kind of business does the speaker work for?

説明文についての設問に対し、最も適切なものを1つずつ選びましょう。

8. What kind of business does the speaker work for?

(A) A construction company　　(B) A travel company

(C) A food company

9. What is the purpose of the phone message?

(A) To change the food order　　(B) To change the drinks order

(C) To cancel the order

Grammar Review 形容詞

形容詞は名詞を修飾する語です。

Jennifer has a **cute** dog.
形容詞　　名詞

形容詞cuteを名詞dogの前に置いて、どのような犬かを説明しています。

１．名詞の前に置いて、後ろの名詞を修飾するのが最も一般的な形で、**beautiful** flower, **big** house, **small** cat, **brown** eyes, **quiet** girl, **wonderful** weather, のようになります。

２．be 動詞の後ろに置いて、その名詞（主語）がどのようであるか説明する形もあります。

Robert is so **kind.**
名詞　　　　　形容詞

主語の名詞 Robert がどのような人なのか、be 動詞の後ろに置いて説明しています。

Mary is **loud**. / John is **tall**. / The story is **interesting**. のようになります。

３．名詞の後ろに置く形容詞には、動詞の目的語を修飾するものもあります。

David makes me **sad.**
名詞　　形容詞

動詞 makes の目的語である me を説明しています。（David は私を悲しくさせる）

< 例題 > 各空所に入れるべき最も適切な語を１つずつ選びなさい。

① Emily bought some ------- flowers at the shop.

　(A) beauty　(B) beautiful　(C) beautifully

② These old papers are -------.

　(A) important　(B) importance　(C) importantly

③ The TV show made me so -------.

　(A) happy　(B) happiness　(C) happily

Hop UNIT 1~UNIT 5

Step UNIT 6~UNIT 9

Jump UNIT 10~UNIT 14

PART 5 短文穴埋め問題

> **Check Point!**
> 文法問題：形容詞、語彙問題：名詞
> 空所の後の名詞を修飾するのは「形容詞」であることを見極めましょう。

それぞれの空所に入れるのに最も適切なものを1つずつ選びましょう。

10. When writing a business letter, you should use ------- language.

    (A) form   (B) formal   (C) formality

11. Sarah wrote an e-mail to the customer in a very ------- way.

    (A) polite   (B) politely   (C) politeness

12. When writing an e-mail, it is important to write a clear -------.

    (A) impression   (B) object   (C) subject

13. Our manager always says that a quick ------- is important in business communication.

    (A) letter   (B) response   (C) paper

PART 6　長文穴埋め問題

Check Point!　Letter
文法問題：形容詞、語彙問題：動詞

それぞれの空所に入れるのに最も適切なものを1つずつ選びましょう。

Dear Ms. Young,

Thank you for your interest in our products.

I will be able to visit your office to ------- you our latest BRW 3000 laptop
            14.
computer. Please let me know a ------- date and time for you. I am going
                              15.
on a business trip to Canada for two weeks at the beginning of next
month, so I would like to visit you sometime this month.

I am looking forward to your reply.

Kind regards,

Tom Moore
Sales Team
Archway Computers

---

14. (A) find
    (B) show
    (C) decide

15. (A) convenient
    (B) right
    (C) useful

Check Point! Letter—1つの文書
差出人、受取人、には常に目を通しましょう。

文章を読んで、それぞれの設問の答えとして最も適切なものを1つずつ選びましょう。

To whom it may concern,

I am writing to apply to be a volunteer helper for the City Marathon.

I was a runner in the third and fifth City Marathons, so I know a lot about the race. I also know how important volunteers are. The volunteers helped me a lot when I was in the race. Now I would like to help others.

I am available for the whole weekend and I am happy to help with any task.

I look forward to hearing from you.

Yours sincerely,

Michael Robinson

16. What is the purpose of the letter?

(A) To promote the marathon

(B) To apply to be a volunteer

(C) To enter the City Marathon

17. What is true about Mr. Robinson?

(A) He was a volunteer.

(B) He helped a lot of people.

(C) He was a runner.

Hop
UNIT 1~UNIT 5

Step
UNIT 6~UNIT 9

Jump
UNIT 10~UNIT 14

:: Warm up · Dictation Practice · 🔊 1-62

それぞれの空所に入る語を、音声を聞いて書き入れてみましょう。

1. Please ( )( ) of yourself.

2. I'm going ( )( ) go running.

3. I heard a ( )( ) green tea is very healthy.

4. We finally reached the ( )( ) the mountain.

> 🔍 **Points to Dictate**
>
> 空所には1語ずつ入ります。ナチュラルスピードで発話されるとそれぞ
> れ「テイケア」「アウル」「カッパ」「トッパ」のように聞こえます。

✅ **頻出単語チェック!**

品詞に注意しながら、各語句の意味を選びましょう。

1. exercise ( )　　　　(A) ～にアクセスする

2. rest ( )　　　　　　(B) ダイエット中で

3. athlete ( )　　　　　(C) 休息

4. on a diet ( )　　　　(D) ～を必要とする

5. require [動詞] ( )　　(E) 健康診断

6. medical checkup ( )　(F) 運動

7. access [動詞] ( )　　(G) 頭痛

8. headache ( )　　　　(H) 運動選手

PART 1　写真描写問題　1-63, 64

> *Check Point!* 　人物の動作について説明される問題を見てみましょう。
> A man is ～ ing a bicycle.

それぞれの写真について、3つの説明文のうち適切なものを1つずつ選びましょう。

1.

Ⓐ Ⓑ Ⓒ

2.

Ⓐ Ⓑ Ⓒ

PART 2　応答問題　1-65-67

> *Check Point!* 　頻出の疑問文による質問文を見てみましょう。
> Is Dr. Smith in today?

それぞれの質問の応答として最も適切なものを1つずつ選びましょう。

3. Mark your answer on your answer sheet.　Ⓐ Ⓑ Ⓒ

4. Mark your answer on your answer sheet.　Ⓐ Ⓑ Ⓒ

5. Mark your answer on your answer sheet.　Ⓐ Ⓑ Ⓒ

PART 3   会話問題   1-68, 69

> *Check Point!*   まず「何が話されているのか」大きく捉えましょう。
> What are the speakers discussing?

会話についての設問に対し、最も適切なものを1つずつ選びましょう。

6. What are the speakers discussing?

(A) Going shopping

(B) Running for half an hour

(C) Exercising at the gym

7. What will the man most likely do next?

(A) Run at the gym

(B) Swim at the gym

(C) Have a rest

PART 4   説明文問題   1-70, 71

> *Check Point!*   ラジオ放送です。話をしている人の「職業」は何か聞き取りましょう。
> Who is Kevin White?

説明文についての設問に対し、最も適切なものを1つずつ選びましょう。

8. Who is Kevin White?

(A) The owner of a fitness club   (B) A radio announcer

(C) An athlete

9. What does the speaker encourage listeners to do?

(A) Visit a Web site   (B) Swim in the pool

(C) Come to City Hall

Hop UNIT 1~UNIT 5

Step UNIT 6~UNIT 9

Jump UNIT 10~UNIT 14

Grammar Review　前置詞（時・期間）

前置詞は名詞（代名詞）の前に置いて、その語と文の中の他の語との関係を示す語です。ここでは前置詞の中でも時と期間を表すものに焦点を当てます。まぎらわしい at - on - in と for - during - through を見てみましょう。

■ at - on - in の違い

1．時点、時節、年齢を表す **at**
   時点：**at** 10:00, **at** night, **at** first, **at** the same time
   時節：**at** Christmas, **at** the end of August
   年齢：**at** the age of 17

2．日付・曜日、特定の朝・昼・晩を表す **on**
   日付・曜日：**on** July 16, **on** Saturday, 特定の朝・昼・晩：**on** Monday morning

3．月、季節、年など期間を表す **in**
   期間：**in** April, **in** winter, **in** my life, **in** the year 2001

at はある 1 点を指すイメージ

■ for - during - through の違い

1．ある不特定の期間（ずっと）を表す **for**
   for three hours, **for** a long time

2．特定の期間の間（ずっと、もしくは一点）を表す **during**
   期間を特定するため、during の直後には所有格の my, his, her, 定冠詞 the がつく。
   during her stay in Tokyo, **during** my trip, **during** the meeting
   ➤I have to draw a picture **during** the spring vacation.
   ☞春休み中のどこかで描く

3．期間全体（を通して）を表す **through**
   through the night, **through** the summer, **through** the lesson
   ➤Ben was studying mathematics **through** the night.
   ☞一晩中数学を勉強していた

< 例題 > 各空所に入れるべき最も適切な語を 1 つずつ選びなさい。

① I will meet my client ------- 10 A.M. tomorrow morning.

　(A) at (B) on (C) in

② I would like to visit Karuizawa ------- summer.

　(A) at (B) on (C) in

③ Ken was writing a sales report ------- the night.

　(A) for (B) in (C) through

Reading Section

PART 5   短文穴埋め問題

Check Point! 文法問題：前置詞（時・期間）、語彙問題：名詞
前置詞なら空所の後の時を表す語句に注意し、適切なもの
を選びましょう。

それぞれの空所に入れるのに最も適切なものを 1 つずつ選びましょう。

10. The company café sells breakfast ------- the morning.

    (A) at   (B) in   (C) with

11. David has been on a diet ------- three years but he never loses weight.

    (A) at   (B) for   (C) on

12. All staff are required to have a medical ------- on Friday morning.

    (A) checkup   (B) problem   (C) center

13. Amy always does some ------- before going to bed.

    (A) health   (B) gym   (C) exercise

Hop
UNIT 1~UNIT 5

Step
UNIT 6~UNIT 9

Jump
UNIT 10~UNIT 14

| Check Point! | Notice
文法問題：前置詞（日付・曜日）、語彙問題：形容詞 |

それぞれの空所に入れるのに最も適切なものを１つずつ選びましょう。

City Medical Center Opened Last Week

After two years of construction, the new City Medical Center opened its doors ------- Tuesday last week. A hospital spokesperson said the
14.
new location of the Medical Center is very convenient for people to access. A new bus takes people from the station to just in front of the ------- entrance to the building. For more information about the City
15.
Medical Center, visit Web site *www.revercity.com/medicalcenter*.

---

14. (A) at

　(B) in

　(C) on

15. (A) last

　(B) main

　(C) other

PART 7　読解問題

Check Point!　Text-Message Chain 一1つの文書
テキストメッセージは親しい仲でやり取りされます。

文章を読んで、それぞれの設問の答えとして最も適切なものを1つずつ選びましょう。

Martha Collins（9:15 A.M.）
Hi. Could you do me a favor?

Patrick Reed（9:16 A.M.）
Sure, Martha. What do you need?

Martha Collins（9:17 A.M.）
I've got a headache this morning, so I don't think I can go to the office today.

Patrick Reed（9:18 A.M.）
Really? That's too bad. Do you need me to do anything for you today?

Martha Collins（9:19 A.M.）
Could you send some company brochures to my clients? The list of clients is on my desk.

Patrick Reed（9:20 A.M.）
No problem. Anything else?

Martha Collins（9:21 A.M.）
That's it. Thanks.

16. Who most likely is Mr. Reed?

(A) A coworker

(B) A doctor

(C) A customer

17. At 9:21 A.M., what does Ms. Collins mean when she writes, "That's it"?

(A) That's all.

(B) That's the correct one.

(C) That's the problem.

8 The Bank & The Post Office

Warm up Dictation Practice   1-72

それぞれの空所に入る語を、音声を聞いて書き入れてみましょう。

1. The bank is (   )(   ) the post office.

2. Please (   )(   ) on that sofa until I call you.

3. Please get off the subway at the (   )(   ) for ABC Bank.

4. Please let me know if you (   )(   ) about your bank account.

🔍 Points to Dictate

空所には1語ずつ入ります。1つ目の語尾と2つ目語頭がつながって「ネクストゥ」「シッダウン」「ネクストップ」「ニーディーテイルス」のように聞こえます。

✅ 頻出単語チェック！

品詞に注意しながら、各語句の意味を選びましょう。

1. withdraw [動詞] (   ) 　　(A) 小包

2. package (   ) 　　(B) 副社長

3. open an account (   ) 　　(C) 支店

4. fill out (   ) 　　(D) 〜を引き出す

5. branch (   ) 　　(E) 書類に記入する

6. vice president (   ) 　　(F) 口座を開設する

7. invoice (   ) 　　(G) 〜を残念に思う

8. regret [動詞] (   ) 　　(H) ＜明細付き＞請求書

Listening Section

PART 1　写真描写問題　 1-73, 74

Check Point!　人物の動作について説明される問題を見てみましょう。
A woman is ～ ing money from the machine.

それぞれの写真について、3つの説明文のうち適切なものを1つずつ選びましょう。

1.

Ⓐ Ⓑ Ⓒ

2.

Ⓐ Ⓑ Ⓒ

PART 2　応答問題　 1-75-77

Check Point!　応答問題では平叙文が投げかけられることもあります。
I'd like to open a new account.

それぞれの質問の応答として最も適切なものを1つずつ選びましょう。

3. Mark your answer on your answer sheet.　Ⓐ Ⓑ Ⓒ

4. Mark your answer on your answer sheet.　Ⓐ Ⓑ Ⓒ

5. Mark your answer on your answer sheet.　Ⓐ Ⓑ Ⓒ

> *Check Point!*　「どこで行われている会話か」を問う別の質問を見てみましょう。
> Where most likely is the conversation taking place?

会話についての設問に対し、最も適切なものを1つずつ選びましょう。

6. Where most likely is the conversation taking place?

(A) At an office　　　　(B) At a bank

(C) At the post office

7. What does the man want to do?

(A) Go to his bank　　　(B) Open an account

(C) Listen to the news

> *Check Point!*　話し手は「どこで働いている人か」注意して聞き取りましょう。
> Where does the speaker most likely work?

説明文についての設問に対し、最も適切なものを1つずつ選びましょう。

8. Where does the speaker most likely work?

(A) At a restaurant　　(B) At a hotel　　(C) At a bank

9. What does the speaker mean when he says, "please give him a big hand"?

(A) He wants people to pat him on the shoulder.

(B) He wants people to clap.

(C) He wants people to give him a present.

Grammar Review 前置詞（所属・関連）

「所属・関連」を表す前置詞 **of, from, about, on**

1．A **of** B「Bの一部であるA」や「Bに所属するA」のように **of** は所属を表します。

<u>The capital</u> **of** <u>Japan</u> is Tokyo.
　A　　　　　　B

B（日本）のA（首都）は東京だ
この場合B＞Aの関係が成り立ちます。

2．**from** には「〜の」という「所属」を表す働きがあります。
This is Mr. Peter Landers **from** ABC company.
（こちら ABC 社の Peter Landers さんです）
I am Maria Walker **from** ABC company.
（私は ABC 社の Maria Walker です）
☞第三者を紹介したり、自分を名乗るときに使います。

3．「関連」を表す最も一般的な前置詞は **about** です。
Brian knows a lot **about** Japanese history.
（Brian は日本の歴史についてたくさんの事を知っています）

4．**on** には「関連」を表す働きがあります。
Brian gave us a lecture **on** Japanese history.
（Brian は日本の歴史について私たちに講義しました）

＜例題＞各空所に入れるべき最も適切な語を1つずつ選びなさい。

① I am a member ------- the Human Resources Department.
(A) on   (B) of   (C) with

② Let me introduce you to Barbara Nelson ------- IT Technologies.
(A) on   (B) for   (C) from

③ I would like to buy some books ------- economics.
(A) about (B) at   (C) in

Hop UNIT 1~UNIT 5
Step UNIT 6~UNIT 9
Jump UNIT 10~UNIT 14

PART 5　短文穴埋め問題

Check Point!　文法問題：前置詞（所属・関連）、語彙問題：名詞
前置詞なら空所の後の所属・関連を表す語句に注意して選
びましょう。

それぞれの空所に入れるのに最も適切なものを1つずつ選びましょう。

10. Our new president is Mr. Tim Brown ------- Central Bank.

(A) on　　　　　　(B) at　　　　　　(C) from

11. The head of the city post office, Mike McDonald, talked ------- last year's sales.

(A) at　　　　　　(B) about　　　　　(C) in

12. Paul is worried about how much money is left in his bank -------.

(A) account　　　(B) card　　　　　(C) record

13. Cindy went to the post office to send this month's ------- to the customers.

(A) stamps　　　(B) invoices　　　(C) signatures

PART 6 長文穴埋め問題

Check Point!

Notice
文法問題：前置詞（所属・関連）、語彙問題：副詞

それぞれの空所に入れるのに最も適切なものを1つずつ選びましょう。

Delmore Bank Vine Street Branch is Closing

Dear Customers,

We regret to inform you that we are going to close our Vine Street branch at the end of this month. From next month, users ------- this
14.
branch should visit our Market Street branch, or you can ------- use our
15.
Web site: *www.delmorebankonline.com*. We are very sorry for the inconvenience.

Thank you for your understanding.

Jane Nelson
Branch Manager

14. (A) from
　 (B) of
　 (C) on

15. (A) always
　 (B) almost
　 (C) quite

> **Check Point!**
> Online Chat Discussion － 1つの文書
> 知り合い同士で交わされます。参加者の関係性をキャッチしましょう。

文章を読んで、それぞれの設問の答えとして最も適切なものを1つずつ選びましょう。

< Group Chat ≡

Ken Watson (8:48 A.M.)
Good morning. Have you had a chance to think of any ideas for increasing the number of customers?

Robert Jones (8:48 A.M.)
No, not yet.

Maria Peterson (8:49 A.M.)
How about making a donation to victims of natural disasters? Whenever a customer opens a new account at our bank, we can donate some money to charity.

Robert Jones (8:50 A.M.)
Great idea, Maria. I like it.

Ken Watson (8:50 A.M.)
Yeah, it's a good idea. Let me talk to the other managers in the meeting this afternoon. I hope they like the idea.

Maria Peterson (8:51 A.M.)
Thank you, Ken. Good luck. If you need any help, please ask.

---

16. Where do the writers most likely work?

(A) At a charity
(B) At a bank
(C) At a department store

17. What will Mr. Watson most likely do next?

(A) Open a new account
(B) Ask Ms. Peterson for some help
(C) Attend a meeting

9 New Products

Hop
UNIT 1~UNIT 5

Step
UNIT 6~UNIT 9

Jump
UNIT 10~UNIT 14

:: **Warm up** ▸ **Dictation Practice** 2-01

それぞれの空所に入る語を、音声を聞いて書き入れてみましょう。

1. I (　　　)(　　　) see the latest model as soon as possible.

2. First, we (　　　)(　　　) collect data about our customers.

3. We can develop a new product (　　　)(　　　).

4. We all agreed (　　　)(　　　) decision.

> 🔍 **Points to Dictate**
>
> 空所には１語ずつ入ります。ナチュラルスピードで発話されると前の空
> 所の最後の音と、次の空所の最初の音が１つになって「ウォントゥ」
> 「ニートゥ」「ウィッゼム」「ウィザット」のように聞こえます。

✅ **頻出単語チェック!**

品詞に注意しながら、各語句の意味を選びましょう。

1. chart (　) 　　　　　(A) 研究者

2. latest (　) 　　　　　(B) 図

3. advertisement (　) 　　(C) 会議

4. conference (　) 　　　　(D) 実演する

5. develop [動詞] (　) 　　(E) 最新の

6. researcher (　) 　　　　(F) 広告

7. demonstrate [動詞] (　) (G) 〜を開発する

8. feature (　) 　　　　　(H) 特徴

Listening Section

PART 1　写真描写問題

 2-02, 03

> *Check Point!*　複数の人物の動作について説明される問題を見てみましょう。
> They're ～ ing to a presentation.

それぞれの写真について、3つの説明文のうち適切なものを1つずつ選びましょう。

1.

Ⓐ Ⓑ Ⓒ

2.

Ⓐ Ⓑ Ⓒ

PART 2　応答問題

 2-04-06

> *Check Point!*　応答問題では平叙文が投げかけられることもあります。
> I want the latest model of this hair dryer.

それぞれの質問の応答として最も適切なものを1つずつ選びましょう。

3. Mark your answer on your answer sheet.　Ⓐ Ⓑ Ⓒ

4. Mark your answer on your answer sheet.　Ⓐ Ⓑ Ⓒ

5. Mark your answer on your answer sheet.　Ⓐ Ⓑ Ⓒ

PART 3 会話問題 2-07, 08

> **Check Point!** 「何についてのディスカッションか」大きく捉えましょう。
> What are the speakers mainly discussing?

Hop
UNIT 1~UNIT 5

Step
UNIT 6~UNIT 9

Jump
UNIT 10~UNIT 14

会話についての設問に対し、最も適切なものを1つずつ選びましょう。

6. What are the speakers mainly discussing?

(A) The development of new contact lenses

(B) Ways of advertising a product

(C) A newspaper promotion

7. What problem does the woman mention?

(A) A TV commercial that did not work

(B) An advertisement in the newspapers that did not work

(C) An expensive advertisement that did not work

PART 4 説明文問題 2-09, 10

> **Check Point!** この話は「どこで行われているか」聞き取りましょう。
> Where is the talk taking place?

説明文についての設問に対し、最も適切なものを1つずつ選びましょう。

8. Where is the talk taking place?

(A) At a conference center   (B) At a hotel

(C) At a company

9. What is mentioned about the size of the conference?

(A) It's decreasing.   (B) It's increasing.

(C) It's almost the same as last year.

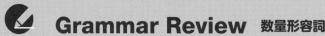

数量形容詞は対象となる**名詞の数や量の多少**を表す形容詞です。

普通の形容詞は「<u>黄色い</u>ハンカチ」、「<u>大きな</u>車」のようにハンカチや車といった名詞を形容してどんなハンカチか車かを表しています。数量形容詞は文字通りその対象となる名詞の数・量を「<u>多い、少ない</u>」「<u>たくさんの、少しの</u>」で言い表します。

一方、形容される名詞には大きく分けて、数えることができる「可算名詞」と数えられない「不可算名詞」があります。

☞可算名詞：apple, box, cat, dictionary, key, pen, tree, etc.

☞不可算名詞：butter, information, meat, milk, water, etc.

そのどちらに使う形容詞か注意が必要です。

以下は代表的な数量形容詞の一覧です。

数量形容詞	数（可算）	量（不可算）
たくさんの	many	much
少しある	a few	a little
ほとんどない	few	little

There are **many** *cats* in my house.　☞たくさんのネコがいる
There is **much** *water* in the pool.　☞たくさんの水が入っている
There are **a few** *cats* in my house.　☞少しのネコがいる
There is **a little** *water* in the pool.　☞少し水が入っている
There are **few** *cats* in my house.　☞ネコはほとんどいない
There is **little** *water* in the pool.　☞水はほとんど入っていない

< 例題 > 各空所に入れるべき最も適切な語を1つずつ選びなさい。

① There are ------- apples on the desk.

(A) many 　　(B) little 　　(C) a little

② Mr. Robinson has ------- information about the festival.

(A) many 　　(B) few 　　(C) a little

③ There is ------- milk in the refrigerator.

(A) a few 　　(B) few 　　(C) little

Reading Section

PART 5 短文穴埋め問題

Check Point! 文法問題：数量形容詞、語彙問題：副詞
対象となる「名詞の数」や「量の多少」を見極めましょう。

それぞれの空所に入れるのに最も適切なものを1つずつ選びましょう。

10. ------- of our new products were developed by the young researchers.

(A) All   (B) Either   (C) Every

11. We will have time to discuss ------- new product at the meeting.

(A) each   (B) few   (C) most

12. The sales report is due tomorrow, so please finish it --------.

(A) easily   (B) quickly   (C) certainly

13. It ------- needs two to three years to develop a new product.

(A) briefly   (B) deeply   (C) usually

動詞や形容詞、他の副詞を修飾する語が副詞です。副詞の代表的な形が形容詞＋lyです。
easi**ly**, happi**ly**, simp**ly**, slow**ly** などです。
修飾される語とともに文の中で意味が通じる副詞を選ぶのがポイントです。

> **Check Point!** Letter
> 文法問題：数量形容詞、語彙問題：動詞

それぞれの空所に入れるのに最も適切なものを1つずつ選びましょう。

Vasel Corporation

333 Green Village Ave.

Los Angeles, CA 67189

Dear Mr. Smith,

Vasel Corporation is attending the New Tech Expo again this year. We are going to ------- several new products, including our new cordless vacuum
14.
cleaner. We will have ------- sample machines at the booth, so please
15.
come and try one for yourself. I am sure you will be impressed.

We look forward to seeing you there.

Sincerely,

Bob Johnson

Sales Manager

Vasel Corporation

---

14. (A) grow   (B) demonstrate   (C) plan

15. (A) a little   (B) much   (C) some

> some ＋名詞　いくつかの特定されていない対象　some books
> some of the+ 名詞　特定された対象のうちのいくつか。

PART 7　読解問題

Check Point!　Article —1つの文書
文挿入問題は前後関係から特定するようにしましょう。

Hop
UNIT 1~UNIT 5

Step
UNIT 6~UNIT 9

Jump
UNIT 10~UNIT 14

文章を読んで、それぞれの設問の答えとして最も適切なものを1つずつ選びましょう。

"Sales Assistant" Wins Software-of-the-Year Award

(December 12)—Web magazine *Soft World* announced that its Software-of-the-Year Award was given to "Sales Assistant" by Zop Software.

—[1]—. *Soft World* explained that "Sales Assistant" has changed the way people do sales. —[2]—. The software manages all the data you need to do sales, such as notes from conversations and records of past business. —[3]—. "Sales Assistant" has sold almost 500,000 copies in just six months.

---

16. What does the article mainly discuss?

(A) The number of sales of the software

(B) The development of the software

(C) The features of the software

17. In which of the positions marked [1], [2], and [3] does the following sentence best belong?

"It can also guess what they will buy next."

(A) [1]

(B) [2]

(C) [3]

10 Travel

⋮⋮ *Warm up* ▏ **Dictation Practice** 2-11

それぞれの空所に入る語を、音声を聞いて書き入れてみましょう。

1. It's the (　　　)(　　　) of the year to travel.

2. I've been to France (　　　)(　　　).

3. I bought (　　)(　　)(　　) souvenirs.

4. (　　　)(　　) people visit this museum every day.

┌─ 🔍 **Points to Dictate** ─┐

空所には1語ずつ入ります。1. と2. は語尾と語頭の /t/ が重なって「ベスタイム」「エイタイムス」と聞こえます。3. と4. は「アラロ」「ロッツア」のように聞こえます。

✅ **頻出単語チェック！**

品詞に注意しながら、各語句の意味を選びましょう。

1. passenger (　　)　　　　　(A) 〜を留める
2. check in [動詞] (　　)　　(B) ＜人を＞車で拾う
3. aboard (　　)　　　　　　　(C) 乗客
4. fasten [動詞] (　　)　　　(D) チェックインする
5. crew (　　)　　　　　　　　(E) 旅行代理店
6. bound for (　　)　　　　　　(F) ＜航空機などに＞乗って
7. travel agency (　　)　　　　(G) 〜行きの
8. pick up (　　)　　　　　　　(H) 乗組員

Listening Section

PART 1　写真描写問題　2-12, 13

Check Point! 　複数の人物の動作について説明される問題を見てみましょう。
Some people are ～ ing on the bus.

それぞれの写真について、4つの説明文のうち適切なものを1つずつ選びましょう。

1.

Ⓐ Ⓑ Ⓒ Ⓓ

2.

Ⓐ Ⓑ Ⓒ Ⓓ

PART 2　応答問題　2-14-16

Check Point! 　頻出の疑問文による質問文を見てみましょう。
How long does it take to get to the airport?

それぞれの質問の応答として最も適切なものを1つずつ選びましょう。

3. Mark your answer on your answer sheet. 　Ⓐ Ⓑ Ⓒ

4. Mark your answer on your answer sheet. 　Ⓐ Ⓑ Ⓒ

5. Mark your answer on your answer sheet. 　Ⓐ Ⓑ Ⓒ

Check Point! 「どこで行われている会話か」聞き取りましょう。
Where does this conversation take place?

会話についての設問に対し、最も適切なものを１つずつ選びましょう。

6. Where does this conversation take place?

(A) At a restaurant

(B) At an airport

(C) At a hotel

7. What is the problem?

(A) He can't find her booking.

(B) She hasn't made a reservation.

(C) The computer is broken.

8. What does the man ask the woman to do?

(A) Spell her family name

(B) Look for something

(C) Make a reservation

PART 4 説明文問題

 2-19, 20

Check Point! 説明文は「誰に向けて話されているものか」聞き取りましょう。
Who is the announcement for?

説明文についての設問に対し、最も適切なものを 1 つずつ選びましょう。

9. Who is the announcement for?

(A) Airport workers

(B) Airline passengers

(C) Airline crew

10. What are passengers asked to do?

(A) Shake a little

(B) Check the travel schedule

(C) Fasten their seatbelts

11. What does the speaker say flight attendants will do soon?

(A) Board Flight 55

(B) Arrive at Los Angeles

(C) Serve dinner

自動詞と**他動詞**を考える際、文型と一緒に考えたほうが効率的です。

■**自動詞**と**他動詞**の見分け方

自動詞は第１文型の S＋V、もしくは第２文型の S＋V＋C で使われています。一方、**他動詞**は後に目的語（名詞）を伴っています。第５文型では目的語である me をどうするという意味で、補語の happy が続いています。

	S	V	O₁	O₂	C	文型
自動詞	I	**run.**				第１
	Betty	**is**			a teacher.	第２
他動詞	I	**like**		dogs.		第３
	Tim	**gave**	me	a present.		第４
	Linda	**made**		me	happy.	第５

この表で見る通り、**自動詞**は目的語を伴いません。**他動詞**は目的語（O）を伴います。目的語はこの表にあるような単純な名詞ばかりとは限りませんが、何らかの目的語を伴うことは覚えておきましょう。

■多くの動詞は**自動詞・他動詞両方**の働きをする

自動詞としてのみ使われる動詞 belong や arrive、他動詞としてのみ使われる動詞 discuss や accept のような動詞はありますが、多くの動詞は両方の働きをします。

➤ 自動詞のみの例

belong to the sales section（営業部に所属している）、**arrive** in London（ロンドンに着く）

➤ 他動詞のみの例

discussed the price（価格を話し合った）、**accept** your offer（申し出を受ける）

➤ 自動詞・他動詞両方の働きをする例

Mark was **running** in the park. ☞公園で走っていた←自動詞

Mark will **run** the company from next month. ☞自分の会社を経営する←他動詞

＜例題＞各空所に入れるべき最も適切な語を１つずつ選びなさい。

① We ------- the hotel.

(A) arrived (B) arrived at (C) arrived to

② The team ------- the new business project.

(A) discussed (B) discussed about (C) discussed of

③ He is ------- a newspaper.

(A) reading (B) reading at (C) reading on

Reading Section

PART 5　短文穴埋め問題

Check Point!　文法問題：自動詞と他動詞、語彙問題：副詞
「目的語のある・なし」で自動詞と他動詞を見極めましょう。

それぞれの空所に入れるのに最も適切なものを1つずつ選びましょう。

12. Ocean Airlines Flight 009 will ------- at Singapore International Airport in 30 minutes.

(A) arrive　　　　(B) depart　　　　(C) fly

13. The team ------- the schedule for their business trip to Korea yesterday.

(A) discussed　　　(B) talked　　　(C) told

14. ------- 500 passengers were on the express train bound for London.

(A) Approximately　(B) Automatically　(C) Slowly

15. This travel agency is ------- good at tours in Europe.

(A) quickly　　　(B) directly　　　(C) especially

それぞれの空所に入れるのに最も適切なものを1つずつ選びましょう。

Faster, Safer Trains

We've been working hard to improve your -------.
  16.

From next month, we will start using our amazing new DF11 trains between Washington D.C. and New York. These trains will reduce travel time by 30 minutes and the braking system is so smooth that you probably won't even ------- it!
  17.

-------.
  18.

---

16. (A) change

(B) road

(C) journey

(D) office

17. (A) notice

(B) notices

(C) noticing

(D) noticed

18. (A) Please come and help.

(B) Please accept my apologies.

(C) Please answer our question.

(D) Please enjoy your journey.

PART 7 説明文問題

Hop
UNIT 1～UNIT 5

Step
UNIT 6～UNIT 9

Jump
UNIT 10～UNIT 14

Check Point! Schedule & E-mail ─2つの文書
「何のスケジュールか」と「Eメールの主旨」を読み取
りましょう。

文章を読んで、それぞれの設問の答えとして最も適切なものを1つずつ選びましょう。

Time	Schedule
12:10 P.M.	Mr. Cheng will pick you up at the airport.
1:00 P.M.	Lunch with Dr. Coe at View Hotel
2:30 P.M.	Meeting with Mr. Wilson at Todd & Bates
3:15 P.M.	Meeting with Ms. Bailey at Hucom
4:45 P.M.	Visit New Tech Exhibition at Florida Trading Center

From: Mary White <mwhite@rajay.com>

To: Donald Long <dlong@rajay.com>

Date: June 14

Subject: Schedule change

Dear Mr. Long,

I am writing to let you know about a change to your schedule tomorrow.

I received an e-mail from Mr. Wilson from Todd & Bates and unfortunately he caught the flu, so he cannot meet you tomorrow afternoon. So, I called Ms. Bailey at Hucom and asked if she was able to meet you at the time you were supposed to meet Mr. Wilson and she kindly agreed. So you will have more time to visit the New Tech Exhibition than originally scheduled.

Please ask if you have any questions.

Have a nice trip,

Mary

19. What is the purpose of the e-mail?

(A) To arrange a meeting

(B) To cancel a meeting

(C) To agree with Mr. Long

(D) To explain a schedule change

20. Who is Mary White?

(A) An employee of Todd & Bates

(B) An employee of Hucom

(C) Mr. Long's secretary

(D) Mr. Wilson's secretary

21. According to the new schedule, when will Mr. Long meet Ms. Bailey?

(A) 1:00 P.M.

(B) 2:30 P.M.

(C) 3:15 P.M.

(D) 4:45 P.M.

11 Daily Life

:: **Warm up**　　　**Dictation Practice** 2-21

それぞれの空所に入る語を、音声を聞いて書き入れてみましょう。

1. Please (　　　　　)(　　　　　　　) at home.

2. This movie always (　　　　　)(　　　　) cry.

3. I will (　　　　)(　　　　　) to the station.

4. It (　　　　　)(　　　　　　) five minutes to get to the bus stop.

> 🔍 **Points to Dictate**
>
> 空所には 1 語ずつ入ります。空所の 2 つの語がつながって別の音になります。それぞれ「メイキヨアセルフ」「メイキシュ」「テイキュ」「テイキシュ」のように聞こえます。

✅ **頻出単語チェック！**

品詞に注意しながら、各語句の意味を選びましょう。

1. repair [動詞] (　　)　　　　　(A) 事故

2. recommend [動詞] (　　)　　　(B) 〜のスケジュールを変更する

3. reschedule [動詞] (　　)　　　(C) 放送

4. broadcast (　　)　　　　　　　(D) フィードバック

5. recipe (　　)　　　　　　　　　(E) 〜を修理する

6. accident (　　)　　　　　　　　(F) ほうび、報酬

7. reward (　　)　　　　　　　　　(G) 〜を薦める

8. feedback (　　)　　　　　　　　(H) レシピ

Hop UNIT 1~UNIT 5

Step UNIT 6~UNIT 9

Jump UNIT 10~UNIT 14

2-22, 23

Check Point!

複数の人物の動作について説明される問題を見てみましょう。
They're ～ ing in the kitchen.

それぞれの写真について、4つの説明文のうち適切なものを1つずつ選びましょう。

1.

Ⓐ Ⓑ Ⓒ Ⓓ

2.

Ⓐ Ⓑ Ⓒ Ⓓ

| PART 2 | 応答問題 |

2-24-26

Check Point!

頻出する疑問文による質問文を見てみましょう。
Would you mind shutting the door?

それぞれの質問の応答として最も適切なものを1つずつ選びましょう。

3. Mark your answer on your answer sheet. Ⓐ Ⓑ Ⓒ

4. Mark your answer on your answer sheet. Ⓐ Ⓑ Ⓒ

5. Mark your answer on your answer sheet. Ⓐ Ⓑ Ⓒ

PART 3　会話問題　 2-27, 28

Check Point!　まず「何についての会話か」大きく捉えましょう。
What is the conversation mainly about?

会話についての設問に対し、最も適切なものを1つずつ選びましょう。

6. What is the conversation mainly about?

(A) Changing the delivery schedule

(B) Recommending some wine

(C) Rescheduling a woman's plans

7. What is the problem?

(A) The food was not frozen.

(B) The delivery schedule doesn't suit her.

(C) They sent the wrong package.

8. What does the man say he will do?

(A) Deliver the package tomorrow

(B) Leave the package by the door

(C) Receive the package today

> *Check Point!* 「何についてのラジオ放送なのか」大きく捉えましょう。
> What is the radio broadcast mainly about?

説明文についての設問に対し、最も適切なものを1つずつ選びましょう。

9. What is the radio broadcast mainly about?

(A) Radio KKB

(B) Shopping

(C) Traffic

10. What does the speaker say is causing a delay?

(A) A sale at the shopping center

(B) Some bridge repairs

(C) An accident

11. What does the speaker advise the drivers to do?

(A) Drive slowly

(B) Take the East Bridge

(C) Not use the East Bridge

Grammar Review　接尾辞と品詞 -- 形容詞

接尾辞と品詞というテーマでは着目点が2つあります。
次の問題を見てみましょう。

> 空所に入れるべき最も適切な語を1つ選びなさい。
> My friend gave me some ------- advice.
> (A) useful　　(B) usefulness　　(C) usefully

■**最初の着目点**は選択肢です。3つの選択肢に共通しているのは useful です。3つの異なる単語から選ばせる語彙問題ではなく、異なる語尾から選択させる品詞問題であることが分かります。

■**着目点その2**は空所の後です。空所の後には advice という名詞があります。名詞を修飾するのは形容詞ですので、空所には形容詞を選ぶのが正解です。

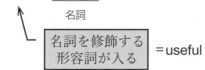

My friend gave me some ------- <u>advice.</u>
名詞

名詞を修飾する
形容詞が入る　=useful

-ful は形容詞を作る接尾辞で、-ness は名詞を、-ly は副詞を作ります。

では形容詞を作る接尾辞を知ることが大切ですが、以下が代表的なものです。
-able（comfort**able**/ 快適な）, -ar（cle**ar**/ 明快な）, -ative（neg**ative**/ 否定的な）, -ese（Japan**ese**/ 日本の）, -ful（beauti**ful**/ 美しい）, -ic（automat**ic**/ 自動の）, -ish（fool**ish**/ ばかげた）, -ous（danger**ous**/ 危険な）, -ious（ser**ious**/ 重大な）, etc.

< 例題 > 各空所に入れるべき最も適切な語を1つずつ選びなさい。

① I was surprised by his ------- ideas.

　　(A) create　　　(B) creative　　　　(C) creativity

② We heard a ------- sound from outside.

　　(A) mystery　　(B) mysteriously　　(C) mysterious

③ May could buy a mobile phone at a ------- price.

　　(A) reason　　(B) reasonable　　　(C) reasonably

PART 5 短文穴埋め問題

Check Point! 文法問題：接尾辞と品詞—形容詞、語彙問題：形容詞
「選択肢の語尾を見て」形容詞はどれか判断しましょう。

それぞれの空所に入れるのに最も適切なものを1つずつ選びましょう。

12. Their house is in a very ------- location.

(A) attract

(B) attraction

(C) attractive

(D) attractively

13. Recently, we have been eating ------- meals at the Vegetarian Café.

(A) health

(B) healthy

(C) healthfulness

(D) healthfully

14. I really don't like getting on ------- trains every morning.

(A) clouded

(B) clever

(C) crowded

(D) inside

15. We will have ------- rain tomorrow because of the typhoon.

(A) deep

(B) full

(C) heavy

(D) strange

PART 6　長文穴埋め問題

Check Point!　E-mail
文法問題：接尾辞と品詞、語彙問題：接続語句

それぞれの空所に入れるのに最も適切なものを 1 つずつ選びましょう。

To:　　Nancy <nphillips@xmail.com>

From:　Helen Carter <likecarter@jespert.com>

Date:　July 15

Subject:　Thank you!

Hi Nancy,

Thank you so much for helping me set up Barbara's birthday party last night. It was an ------- party and everyone had a great time. -------, the **16.** **17.** spicy chicken you brought was delicious! Could you share the recipe? I was trying to look it up online, but I haven't found it yet. -------. Sorry **18.** to trouble you.

Thank you,

Helen

---

16. (A) amaze

　　 (B) amazing

　　 (C) amazingly

　　 (D) amazement

17. (A) By the way

　　 (B) For example

　　 (C) As a result

　　 (D) On the other hand

18. (A) I found it in a cookbook.

  (B) It's not good for a birthday.

  (C) I want to make it for my family this weekend.

  (D) See you at the party.

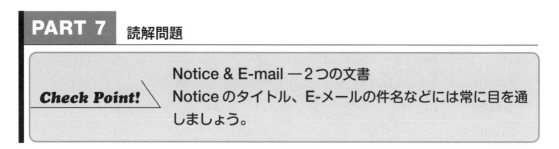

文章を読んで、それぞれの設問の答えとして最も適切なものを1つずつ選びましょう。

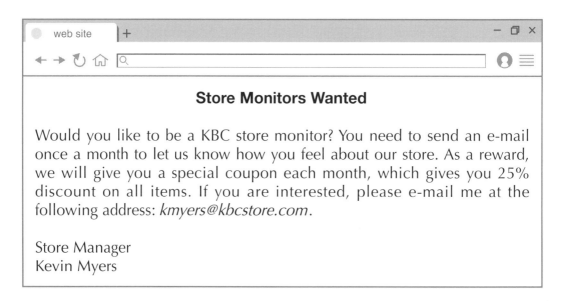

Store Monitors Wanted

Would you like to be a KBC store monitor? You need to send an e-mail once a month to let us know how you feel about our store. As a reward, we will give you a special coupon each month, which gives you 25% discount on all items. If you are interested, please e-mail me at the following address: *kmyers@kbcstore.com*.

Store Manager
Kevin Myers

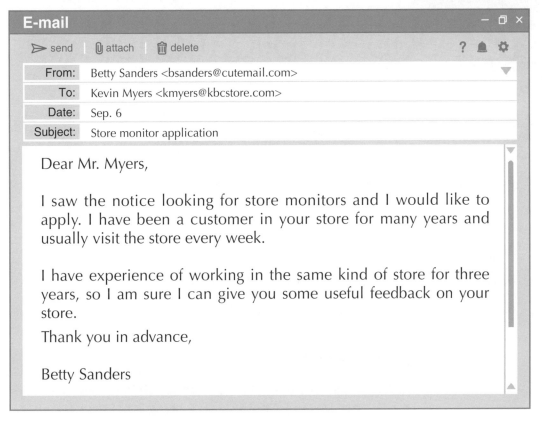

19. What is the purpose of the notice?

(A) To ask for people to become store monitors

(B) To give customers a coupon

(C) To tell customers about a sale

(D) To announce a monthly e-mail newsletter

20. According to the notice, what can a monitor get?

(A) An e-mail

(B) A free item

(C) A reward

(D) A report

21. What is true about Ms. Sanders?

(A) She works for KBC store.

(B) She wants to recruit a store monitor.

(C) She wants to be a store manager.

(D) She wants to be a store monitor.

12 Job Applications

Dictation Practice 2-31

それぞれの空所に入る語を、音声を聞いて書き入れてみましょう。

1. (　　　　　)(　　　　　) come to our office?

2. (　　　　　)(　　　　　) send us your resume?

3. (　　　)(　　　) think you're able to visit us?

4. (　　　)(　　　) attend the interview?

> 🔍 **Points to Dictate**
>
> 空所には1語ずつ入ります。決まりきった表現は省略化して発話されます。ここでは「ウジュ」「クジュ」3. と4. はどちらも「ジュ」「ジュ」のように聞こえます。

✅ **頻出単語チェック！**

品詞に注意しながら、各語句の意味を選びましょう。

1. interview (　　) 　　　　　(A) 申請

2. application (　　) 　　　　(B) 給料

3. resume (　　) 　　　　　(C) ～を探し求める

4. narrow down [動詞] (　　) 　(D) 資格

5. full-time (　　) 　　　　　(E) ～を絞る

6. qualification (　　) 　　　(F) 履歴書

7. seek [動詞] (　　) 　　　　(G) 常勤の

8. salary (　　) 　　　　　　(H) 面接

🎧 Listening Section

PART 1　写真描写問題
 2-32, 33

> **Check Point!** 複数の人物の動作について説明される問題を見てみましょう。
> They're ～ ing with a woman.

それぞれの写真について、4つの説明文のうち適切なものを1つずつ選びましょう。

1.

Ⓐ Ⓑ Ⓒ Ⓓ

2.

Ⓐ Ⓑ Ⓒ Ⓓ

PART 2　応答問題
 2-34-36

> **Check Point!** 頻出の疑問文による質問文を見てみましょう。
> What did you major in at university?

それぞれの質問の応答として最も適切なものを1つずつ選びましょう。

3. Mark your answer on your answer sheet.　　Ⓐ Ⓑ Ⓒ

4. Mark your answer on your answer sheet.　　Ⓐ Ⓑ Ⓒ

5. Mark your answer on your answer sheet.　　Ⓐ Ⓑ Ⓒ

> **Check Point!** 「どこで行われている会話か」聞き取りましょう。
> Where most likely is the conversation taking place?

会話についての設問に対し、最も適切なものを1つずつ選びましょう。

6. Where most likely is the conversation taking place?

(A) At a university

(B) At a library

(C) At a research center

(D) At an office

7. What are the speakers mainly discussing?

(A) Looking for a new office

(B) Hiring a new employee

(C) Talking about a trip

(D) Taking holidays

8. What does the woman mean when she says, "I think we've found a good one"?

(A) She thinks they have found a good product.

(B) She thinks they have found a good person.

(C) She thinks they have found a good holiday.

(D) She thinks they have found a good job.

PART 4　説明文問題　 2-39, 40

Check Point!　まず「聞き手は誰なのか」聞き取りましょう。
Who most likely are the listeners?

説明文についての設問に対し、最も適切なものを1つずつ選びましょう。

9. Who most likely are the listeners?

(A) New employees

(B) Members of the HR team

(C) Online specialists

(D) Trainers

10. What does the company want to do?

(A) Get resumes from five people

(B) Interview three people online

(C) Hire three people

(D) Hire five people

11. What does the speaker mean when he says, "we have to narrow down the list to five people"?

(A) Choose five people

(B) Get five people to make a list

(C) Hire five new people

(D) Give a list to five people

「A は B **よりも**大きい」、「A は B と**同じくらい**の大きさ」、「A は～の中で**一番**大きい」など**比較**は日常生活でも良く使われます。**比較**で多く使われるのは young ⇔ old、big ⇔ small などの**形容詞**と early や slowly などの**副詞**です。

・**形容詞**：Jim is <u>young</u>.（Jim は若い）

・**副詞**：Mary walks <u>slowly</u>.（Mary はゆっくり歩く）

■比較の作りかた

比較は**形容詞や副詞の語形を変化**させて作ります。

原　級：語形を変化させる前の元の形例えば young が原級です。

比較級：2 つのものを比べ、「～より若い」というときは、語尾に -er を付けて young**er** とします。文中では比較する対象の前に **than** を置いて「○○より若い」とします。

最上級：何人もいる中で「～で最も若い」というときは、語尾に -est を付けて young**est** とします。さらに「最も若い」のは 1 人しかいないので、定冠詞 **the** を付けます。

原　級：Jim is <u>young</u>.（Jim は若い）

比較級：Jim is <u>young**er**</u> **than** Robert.（Jim は Robert より若い）

最上級：Jim is **the** <u>young**est**</u> in his company.（Jim は会社で一番若い）

➤Jim と Robert が「同い年」の場合は原級 young を as…as ではさみ、Jim is **as** <u>young</u> **as** Robert.（Jim と Robert は同い年）とします。

< 例題 > 各空所に入れるべき最も適切な語を 1 つずつ選びなさい。

① Ken's laptop computer is ------- than mine.

    (A) new   (B) newer   (C) newest

② Meeting Room #3 is the ------- on the third floor.

    (A) big   (B) bigger   (C) biggest

③ Our company's building is as ------- as ABC Bank next door.

    (A) tall   (B) taller   (C) tallest

Reading Section

PART 5 短文穴埋め問題

> **Check Point!** 文法問題：比較、語彙問題：形容詞
> 比較表現を作る単語（**than** など）がないか注意しましょう。

それぞれの空所に入れるのに最も適切なものを 1 つずつ選びましょう。

12. Magnum Corporation pays ------- wages than C&W Inc.

    (A) higher   (B) high

    (C) highest   (D) much high

13. These days, companies are contacting applicants ------- than before.

    (A) quick   (B) quickly

    (C) more quickly   (D) most quickly

14. I am looking for a ------- position in the accounting section.

    (A) past   (B) small

    (C) popular   (D) full-time

15. If you are ------- at 2 P.M. next Thursday, please come to our office.

    (A) busy   (B) available

    (C) useful   (D) absent

それぞれの空所に入れるのに最も適切なものを 1 つずつ選びましょう。

Mariab Corporation

11 Winter Street

Acton, MA 98765

Dear Mr. Green,

Thank you for attending the ------- **16.** last Thursday. Your work experience and educational background were far ------- **17.** than we expected. Therefore, we would like to offer you a job as section chief in the sales department. If you wish to accept our offer, please call me and come to the office at 9 A.M. next Monday. -------**18.**.

I'm looking forward to seeing you soon.

Yours sincerely,

Donna Burton

Human Resource Department

Mariab Corporation

16. (A) exhibition

   (B) interview

   (C) job

   (D) conference

17. (A) good

   (B) better

   (C) best

   (D) the best

18. (A) I hope I can get a job.

   (B) I hope you can attend the interview.

   (C) I hope you are well.

   (D) I hope you will accept our offer.

PART 7   読解問題

Check Point! Web page & E-mail ― 2つの文書
ウェブ情報はおおよそ何についてのメッセージかを読み取りましょう。

文章を読んで、それぞれの設問の答えとして最も適切なものを1つずつ選びましょう。

http://www.eastwestair.com

About us | Ticket Reservation | Services | Recruitment

Wanted: Flight Attendants
Qualifications: College Graduate, Fluent in Japanese or Chinese
Route: International Flights to East Asia
Number of positions: 20
Please send your resume by e-mail to the following address:
cnelson@eastwestair.com.

Recruitment Manager
Carol Nelson

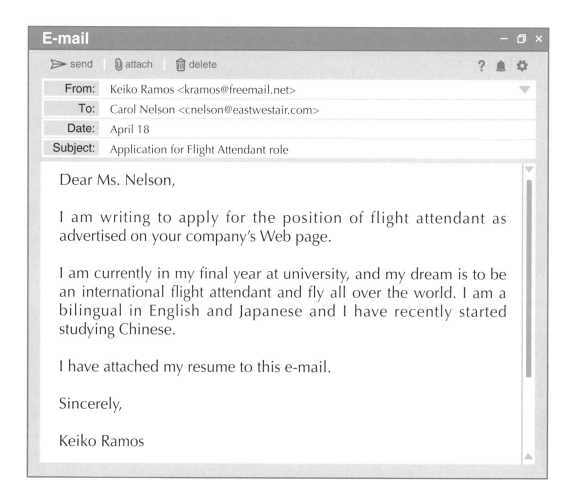

E-mail — ☐ ✕

✉ send   📎 attach   🗑 delete   ? 🔔 ⚙

From: Keiko Ramos <kramos@freemail.net>

To: Carol Nelson <cnelson@eastwestair.com>

Date: April 18

Subject: Application for Flight Attendant role

Dear Ms. Nelson,

I am writing to apply for the position of flight attendant as advertised on your company's Web page.

I am currently in my final year at university, and my dream is to be an international flight attendant and fly all over the world. I am a bilingual in English and Japanese and I have recently started studying Chinese.

I have attached my resume to this e-mail.

Sincerely,

Keiko Ramos

19. What is NOT stated on the Eastwest Airlines Web site?

(A) The number of people they need

(B) The qualifications needed

(C) The languages required

(D) The salary

20. What is the purpose of the e-mail?

(A) To explain about the work of a flight attendant

(B) To tell someone about a job advertisement

(C) To apply for a job

(D) To offer someone a job

21. What is suggested about Ms. Ramos?

(A) She works for Eastwest Airlines.

(B) She can speak two languages.

(C) She is in the second year of university.

(D) She is fluent in Chinese.

Hop
UNIT 1~UNIT 5

Step
UNIT 6~UNIT 9

Jump
UNIT 10~UNIT 14

13 Shopping

Warm up **Dictation Practice** 2-41

それぞれの空所に入る語を、音声を聞いて書き入れてみましょう。

1. Please don't (　　　　)(　　　　) chance.

2. Please take the mall map in (　　　　)(　　　　) get lost.

3. (　　　　)(　　　　) take you to the shop.

4. Please take as much (　　　　)(　　　　) like.

> 🔍 **Points to Dictate**
>
> 空所には1語ずつ入ります。空所の2つの語がつながって別の音になります。それぞれ「ミシュア」「ケイシュ」「レミ」「アジュ」のように聞こえます。

✅ **頻出単語チェック！**

品詞に注意しながら、各語句の意味を選びましょう。

1. enter [動詞] (　　) 　　　　(A) 値札

2. cashier (　　) 　　　　(B) ～を交換する

3. price tag (　　) 　　　　(C) ～を割引する

4. exchange [動詞] (　　) 　　　　(D) 領収書

5. receipt (　　) 　　　　(E) 送料無料

6. saving (　　) 　　　　(F) レジ係

7. discount [動詞] (　　) 　　　　(G) 節約

8. free shipping (　　) 　　　　(H) ～に入る

Listening Section

PART 1　写真描写問題

 2-42, 43

Check Point!　人物の動作について説明される問題を見てみましょう。
A customer is 〜 ing a shopping cart.

それぞれの写真について、4つの説明文のうち適切なものを1つずつ選びましょう。

1.

Ⓐ Ⓑ Ⓒ Ⓓ

2.

Ⓐ Ⓑ Ⓒ Ⓓ

PART 2　応答問題

 2-44-46

Check Point!　頻出の疑問文による質問文を見てみましょう。
How much is this T-shirt?

それぞれの質問の応答として最も適切なものを1つずつ選びましょう。

3. Mark your answer on your answer sheet.　　Ⓐ Ⓑ Ⓒ

4. Mark your answer on your answer sheet.　　Ⓐ Ⓑ Ⓒ

5. Mark your answer on your answer sheet.　　Ⓐ Ⓑ Ⓒ

Hop UNIT 1〜UNIT 5

Step UNIT 6〜UNIT 9

Jump UNIT 10〜UNIT 14

Check Point! 「どこで行われている会話か」聞き取りましょう。
Where most likely are the speakers?

会話についての設問に対し、最も適切なものを１つずつ選びましょう。

6. Where most likely are the speakers?

   (A) At a flower shop

   (B) At a shoe shop

   (C) At a department store

   (D) At a train station

7. What does the woman ask the man about?

   (A) Directions

   (B) Shoes

   (C) The exit

   (D) A price

8. What does the man mean when he says, "You can't miss it"?

   (A) He thinks the woman may make a mistake.

   (B) He hopes the woman can find the shoe store.

   (C) He doesn't know the place either.

   (D) He is sure the woman can find the place.

PART 4　説明文問題

Check Point!　説明文の「主旨」を大きく捉えましょう。
Why is the store having a sale?

説明文についての各設問に対し、最も適切なものを 1 つずつ選びましょう。

9. Why is the store having a sale?

(A) To celebrate an anniversary

(B) To introduce a new cake shop

(C) To sell cheesecake

(D) To show customers some new products

10. Look at the graphic. What is the discount on today's featured item?

(A) 20%

(B) 30%

(C) 40%

(D) 50%

Today's Discounts	
Beef	20% off
Cereal	30% off
Strawberries	40% off
Cheesecake	50% off

11. Where is the list of discounts available?

(A) In the frozen food section

(B) In the vegetable section

(C) At the entrance

(D) At the cake shop

Grammar Review 受動態

受動態の基本形を確認しておきましょう。

■能動態から受動態の作り方

A young lady　bought　the diamond ring.
　　主語　　　　動詞　　　　目的語

（若い女性がそのダイヤモンドの指輪を買った）

The diamond ring　was　bought　by　a young lady.
　　主語　　　　be動詞　過去分詞　by　行為をした人

（そのダイヤモンドの指輪は若い女性によって買われた）

☞主語と目的語が入れ替わり、主語は行為者として by の後に来ます。

■「by＋行為をした人（物）」を使わない受動態

行為をした人（物）が分からない場合や一般の人の場合、by 以下は省略されます。

➤They built the bridge 10 years ago. ⇒ The bridge was built 10 years ago.

（彼らは 10 年前に橋を築いた）⇒（その橋は 10 年前に築かれた）

➤They speak English in the United States. ⇒ English is spoken in the United States.

（人々は合衆国で英語を話している）⇒（英語は合衆国で話されている）

< 例題 > 各空所に入れるべき最も適切な語を 1 つずつ選びなさい。

① This essay was ------- by a famous writer.

(A) write　(B) wrote　(C) written

② Tim was ------- by the dog.

(A) attack　(B) attacked　(C) attacking

③ Is English ------- in the United States?

(A) speak　(B) spoken　(C) speaking

◎受動態の疑問文と否定文（be 動詞＋過去分詞を確認しよう）
　・Is Italian spoken in Canada?
　　（カナダではイタリア語は話されていますか）
　・When was this picture drawn?
　　（この絵はいつ描かれましたか）
　・The building wasn't cleaned yesterday.
　　（昨日そのビルは清掃されませんでした）

Reading Section

PART 5　短文穴埋め問題

> **Check Point!**
>
> 文法問題：受動態、語彙問題：形容詞
> 受動態は「be 動詞＋過去分詞」であることを確認しましょう。

それぞれの空所に入れるのに最も適切なものを１つずつ選びましょう。

12. The oldest department store in our town ------- in 1845.

(A) built　　　　　　(B) building

(C) was built　　　 (D) was build

13. This green sweater was designed ------- world-famous designer Tim Frankl.

(A) by　　　　　　　(B) on

(C) at　　　　　　　(D) with

14. The woman asked the sales assistant to show her the same T-shirt but in a ------- color.

(A) bigger　　　　　(B) cheaper

(C) difficult　　　 (D) different

15. Many people like to buy things at the ------- supermarket because it's convenient.

(A) local　　　　　　(B) quiet

(C) near　　　　　　(D) open

> **Check Point!**　Online message
> 文法問題：受動態、語彙問題：形容詞

それぞれの空所に入れるのに最も適切なものを1つずつ選びましょう。

BK Online Store

Welcome to our online store! This month we are celebrating our fifth anniversary, so to thank our customers, each week many products will be -------. This week's featured item is Smart Air 11 running shoes – the latest
16.
shoes from Sports Tech. You can only find these ------- shoes in our online
17.
store. And, if you buy two pairs, you can get the second pair for half price. -------. So, you can buy a pair for your family or friends. Don't miss
18.
this great offer!

---

16. (A) discount　　(B) discounts

(C) discounting　　(D) discounted

17. (A) gentle　　(B) worse

(C) wonderful　　(D) natural

18. (A) You can also order three pairs.

(B) You can order two different sizes.

(C) You can visit our shop to try them on.

(D) You can keep both pairs for yourself.

PART 7 読解問題

Check Point! 広告 & ショッピングカート & E-mail ―3つの文書
3つの文書にざっと目を通し、それぞれの関係性を把握
しましょう。

文章を読んで、それぞれの設問の答えとして最も適切なものを1つずつ選びましょう。

Hop
UNIT 1~UNIT 5

Step
UNIT 6~UNIT 9

Jump
UNIT 10~UNIT 14

http://www.themellowstyle.com

THE MELLOW STYLE

Winter Sale

from Jan. 10 to Feb. 5

<u>20%-70% off</u>

Buy more than two items and get free shipping

Your Shopping Cart

Item	Size	Color	Price	Discount	Number	Price
Sweater	M	White	$340	40%	1	$204
Jeans	M	Blue	$230	50%	1	$115
Shirt	M	White	$95	20%	2	$152
					Total	$471

```
┌─────────────────────────────────────────────────────────────────┐
│  »»»»      E-mail    «««««                              ⊠         │
├──────────┬────────────────────────────────────────────────────────┤
│ From:    │ Bill Hogan <bhogan@globe.net>                           │
│ To:      │ Customer service <cs.themellowstyle@tms.com>            │
│ Date:    │ Jan. 12                                                 │
│ Subject: │ Change to my order                                      │
├──────────┴────────────────────────────────────────────────────────┤
│  Dear Sir or Madam,                                                │
│                                                                    │
│  I am writing to ask you to make a change to an order I made this  │
│  morning. I ordered a sweater, two shirts and a pair of jeans, but I│
│  would like you to cancel the jeans. Sorry for the last-minute     │
│  change.                                                           │
│                                                                    │
│  Thank you for your help,                                          │
│                                                                    │
│  Bill Hogan                                                        │
└─────────────────────────────────────────────────────────────────┘
```

19. What is the purpose of the advertisement?

    (A) To advertise a holiday on a ship

    (B) To announce a winter sale

    (C) To tell people when the store will be closed

    (D) To promote some new clothes

20. Why is Mr. Hogan writing the e-mail?

    (A) He wants to buy a sweater.

    (B) He wants to buy a pair of jeans.

    (C) He wants to cancel part of his order.

    (D) He wants to thank the store for his order.

21. What amount will be removed from the total?

    (A) $115

    (B) $152

    (C) $230

    (D) $471

14 Education

Hop
UNIT 1~UNIT 5

Step
UNIT 6~UNIT 9

Jump
UNIT 10~UNIT 14

:: **Warm up** > **Dictation Practice** 2-51

それぞれの空所に入る語を、音声を聞いて書き入れてみましょう。

1. I'll (　　　)(　　　) at the training center.

2. I (　　　)(　　　) finish writing the report first.

3. I (　　　)(　　　) that I will teach you economics.

4. He's going to teach business English (　　　)(　　　).

> 🔍 **Points to Dictate**
>
> 空所には1語ずつ入ります。空所の2つの語がつながって別の音になります。それぞれ「ミーチャ」「ワナ」「プロミシュ」「ディシャー」のように聞こえます。

✓ 頻出単語チェック！

品詞に注意しながら、各語句の意味を選びましょう。

1. sales promotion (　) 　　　　(A) 秘訣

2. manager (　) 　　　　(B) 登録を申し込む

3. attitude (　) 　　　　(C) 販売促進活動

4. sales (　) 　　　　(D) 態度

5. remind [動詞] (　) 　　　　(E) 部長

6. tips (　) 　　　　(F) ＜人＞に思い出させる

7. ability (　) 　　　　(G) 販売の

8. sign up [動詞] (　) 　　　　(H) 力量

PART 1　写真描写問題　 2-52, 53

> **Check Point!**　人物以外が主語になっている問題例を見てみましょう。
> The room is not full of students.

それぞれの写真について、4つの説明文のうち適切なものを1つずつ選びましょう。

1.

Ⓐ Ⓑ Ⓒ Ⓓ

2.

Ⓐ Ⓑ Ⓒ Ⓓ

PART 2　応答問題　 2-54-56

> **Check Point!**　頻出の疑問文による質問文を見てみましょう。
> Where did Mr. Kato go to university?

それぞれの質問の応答として最も適切なものを1つずつ選びましょう。

3. Mark your answer on your answer sheet.　　Ⓐ Ⓑ Ⓒ

4. Mark your answer on your answer sheet.　　Ⓐ Ⓑ Ⓒ

5. Mark your answer on your answer sheet.　　Ⓐ Ⓑ Ⓒ

PART 3 会話問題

 2-57, 58

Check Point! 「何についての会話か」、さらに何の「図表」か理解しましょう。
What is the conversation mainly about?

会話についての設問に対し、最も適切なものを1つずつ選びましょう。

6. What is the conversation mainly about?

(A) A schedule change

(B) A business trip

(C) A sales training program

(D) An important meeting

7. What is the man unable to do?

(A) Take the course on Thursday

(B) Train his coworker

(C) Go to London

(D) Meet his clients

8. Look at the graphic. What training course will the man miss?

(A) Introductory Session

(B) E-mailing Clients

(C) Visiting Clients

(D) Sales Techniques Workshop

Sales Training Schedule	
Mon	Introductory Session
Tue	E-mailing Clients
Wed	Visiting Clients
Thu	Sales Techniques Workshop

Check Point! 説明文は「誰に向けて」話されているものか聞き取りましょう。
Who are the listeners?

説明文についての設問に対し、最も適切なものを1つずつ選びましょう。

9. Who are the listeners?

(A) Vice presidents

(B) Company staff

(C) New employees

(D) Section managers

10. What is the main topic of the talk?

(A) The work of each section

(B) A training schedule

(C) The names of managers

(D) The company's history

11. According to the speaker, what will happen at the end of the day?

(A) A history lecture

(B) A coffee break

(C) A discussion

(D) A cocktail party

Grammar Review 接続詞（相関接続詞）

2つの語句をセットにして接続詞の働きをするものを**相関接続詞**と言います。
英語でも日本語と同様に決まった言い方がありますのでまとめてみます。

■相関接続詞の例

both A **and** B	（A も B も両方とも）
either A **or** B	（A か B のどちらか）
not only A **but also** B	（A ばかりでなく B も）
A **as well as** B	（B だけでなく A も）
neither A **nor** B	（A も B もどちらも～ない）

■相関接続詞で結ばれた主語を受ける動詞は、どれが本当の主語かを見つけて判断します。

1. **Both** Tom **and** Maria are going to attend the meeting. ⇒動詞は複数扱い
   （Tom も Maria も会議に参加するつもりです）
2. **Either** Tom **or** Maria is going to attend the meeting. ⇒動詞は B に一致させる
   （Tom か Maria のどちらかが会議に参加するつもりです）
3. **Not only** Tom **but also** Maria is going to attend the meeting. ⇒動詞は B に一致させる
   （Tom ばかりでなく Maria も会議に参加するつもりです）
4. Tom **as well as** Maria is going to attend the meeting. ⇒動詞は A に一致させる
   （Maria だけでなく Tom も会議に参加するつもりです）
5. **Neither** Tom **nor** Maria is going to attend the meeting. ⇒動詞は B に一致させる
   （Tom も Maria も会議に参加するつもりはありません）

➤ 相関接続詞が結びつける A と B は普通文中の対等の要素です。

・～ not only in Japan but also in Korea.
・Either the president or his secretary ～ .

< 例題 > 各空所に入れるべき最も適切な語を1つ選びなさい。

① Either you or I ------- wrong.

   (A) be　　(B) am　　　(C) are

② ------- Charles nor Betty was at the meeting room.

   (A) Both　(B) Either　(C) Neither

③ Paul as well as his parents ------- going to Canada.

   (A) be　　(B) is　　　(C) are

PART 5 短文穴埋め問題

Check Point! 文法問題：相関接続詞、語彙問題：形容詞
「相関接続詞」を構成する単語に目をつけましょう。

それぞれの空所に入れるのに最も適切なものを１つずつ選びましょう。

12. You can take ------- a language course and a business course at the same time.

    (A) both   (B) either

    (C) as   (D) all

13. ------- eating nor drinking is allowed during the workshop.

    (A) Either   (B) Neither

    (C) Unless   (D) Whether

14. It's important to have a ------- attitude during the seminar.

    (A) light   (B) positive

    (C) smooth   (D) full

15. The new employees will have ------- training for business communication.

    (A) main   (B) wide

    (C) past   (D) basic

PART 6   長文穴埋め問題

Check Point!
E-mail
文法問題：相関接続詞、語彙問題：名詞

それぞれの空所に入れるのに最も適切なものを1つずつ選びましょう。

To: Sales Team

From: Bill Martinez

Date: November 30

Subject: Training for Sales People

Dear All,

I am writing to remind you about the sales techniques ------- that will 16. be held next week. -------. As you may know, he was the top car 17. salesman for Stella Cars for over ten years. I'm sure he will share a lot of great tips with us. ------- a manager or an assistant manager from 18. each section should attend.

Please let me know if you have any questions.

Best regards,

Bill

---

16. (A) information

(B) school

(C) workshop

(D) tour

Hop UNIT 1~UNIT 5

Step UNIT 6~UNIT 9

Jump UNIT 10~UNIT 14

17. (A) You will learn some very useful techniques.

(B) Everyone must attend this session.

(C) The trainer will be Roger Torres.

(D) It will take about two hours.

18. (A) Either

(B) Neither

(C) Not only

(D) Both

PART 7　読解問題

Check Point!　E-メール & スケジュール & E-メール ― 3つの文書
3つの文書にざっと目を通し、それぞれの関係性を把握しましょう。

各文章を読んで、それぞれの設問の答えとして最も適切なものを1つずつ選びましょう。

From:　　　HR Department <hrdep@eurotrading.com>

To:　　　All Staff

Date:　　　February 1

Subject:　Language Training

Dear All,

I am pleased to announce that language classes for this year will start at the beginning of March.

As you know, the ability to speak a foreign language is key to keeping a good relationship with our customers. So I hope that everyone will sign up for classes. Please choose the language you need to use with your customers.

Please reply by February 20 to tell me which class you wish to sign up for.

Best regards,

Sandy Cooper

Human Resources Department

Language Training Schedule

Day	8:00-9:30 A.M.	5:00-6:30 P.M.	6:30-8:00 P.M.
Mon.	#M1 Basic French	#M2 Basic Italian	#M3 Basic German
Tue.	#T1 Intermediate Spanish	#T2 Intermediate French	#T3 Intermediate Italian
Wed.	#W1 Advanced Japanese	#W2 Advanced French	#W3 Advanced German
Thu.	#U1 Intermediate German	#U2 Basic Spanish	#U3 Intermediate Japanese
Fri.	#F1 Basic Japanese	#F2 Advanced Italian	#F3 Advanced Spanish

---

From: Keith Watson <kwatson@eurotrading.com>

To: Sandy Cooper <hrdep@eurotrading.com>

Date: February 2

Subject: Language Training

Dear Sandy,

Thank you for the e-mail and language training schedule.

I would like to take the Intermediate Japanese class, but unfortunately, I have a regular online meeting with my client in Osaka every Thursday evening. Is it possible for me to take the Basic class instead?

Thank you for your help.

Best regards,

Keith Watson

19. What is indicated in the first e-mail?

(A) People have to go to a language school.

(B) The company does language training every year.

(C) Language training lasts for a year.

(D) Staff can study any language.

20. What is true about the schedule?

(A) There are three languages that people can choose.

(B) Intermediate Italian class is on Tuesday.

(C) There is a Japanese class on Monday.

(D) There is a French class on Thursday.

21. According to the schedule, what is the most likely class code that Mr. Watson will use?

(A) #M1

(B) #W1

(C) #U3

(D) #F1

Hop
UNIT 1~UNIT 5

Step
UNIT 6~UNIT 9

Jump
UNIT 10~UNIT 14

TEXT PRODUCTION STAFF

edited by	編集
Mitsugu Shishido	宍戸　貢

cover design by	表紙デザイン
Nobuyoshi	藤野伸芳

text design by	本文デザイン
Nobuyoshi	藤野伸芳

CD PRODUCTION STAFF

narrated by	吹き込み者
Dominic Allen (AmE)	ドミニク・アレン (アメリカ英語)
Ann Slater (AmE)	アン・スレーター (アメリカ英語)
Guy Perryman (BrE)	ガイ・ペリマン (イギリス英語))

BEST PRACTICE FOR THE TOEIC® L&R TEST
—Basic—

TOEIC® L&R TESTへの総合アプローチ —ベーシック—

2021年1月20日　初版発行
2022年3月10日　第3刷発行

著　者　吉塚　弘
　　　　Graham Skerritt

発行者　佐野　英一郎

発行所　株式会社 成美堂
　　　　〒101-0052　東京都千代田区神田小川町3-22
　　　　TEL 03-3291-2261　FAX 03-3293-5490
　　　　https://www.seibido.co.jp

印刷・製本　倉敷印刷株式会社

ISBN 978-4-7919-7232-6　　　　　　　　　　　　　Printed in Japan